TRUST STORY

TRUST STORY

Inspiration for Handling Heartbreak

and Facing Your Future

by

PHIL AND KAREN LAZO

Contents

Prologue

Phil

This is a story about "Trust." Yes, trust in God ultimately, but initially about a song with the same name. In 2001, I was inspired to write this song about trusting God with our children, even in unfathomable circumstances. Two years later, we would lose our daughter Lindsay-Grace in a horrific, unexplainable car accident. Realizing the relevance of "Trust" to our situation, I played the song at her memorial service. Soon many people

1

began requesting copies of it. So, we produced a CD project with this song and its story, to have available for anyone who requested one. It has meant so much to us over the years to hear how God has used "Trust" to minister to the hearts of many, including those who have faced personal tragedies. As of 2014, we have given away nearly 4,500 "Trust" CDs coast-to-coast in the United States as well as internationally.

Countless people have continued to express interest in hearing more about our journey in the years after we faced our worst nightmare. This memoir shares some profound lessons we learned and incredible stories of how God worked. Amidst our deepest pain and grief, the Lord was immeasurably faithful in helping us cope with our tragedy, and even find hope, purpose and joy.

Wherever you are in your journey with God, may these stories inspire you to trust Him with even your most precious relationships and challenging circumstances. May these song lyrics also ring true for you:

"Yes Lord, I trust You, no matter how hard it might be.
Yes, Lord, I trust You, even though I'm blind and can't see.
You are my God and You know the way.
No matter what happens, with You I'll stay . . . and trust."

TRUST

a song by Phil Lazo, written February 2001

If I had to choose between my child and my God . . .
And if the Lord said, "Obey and sacrifice."
How would I react? What would I say?
How would I respond? What would I pray?

(CHORUS)
I'd pray, "Yes, Lord, I trust You, no matter how hard it might be.
Yes, Lord, I trust You, even though I'm blind and can't see.
You are my God and You know the way,
No matter what happens, with You I'll stay . . . and trust."

If all my hopes and dreams were somehow stripped away
And if my world collapsed and fear gripped my days—
How would I react, and what would I say?
How would I respond and what would I pray?
(CHORUS)

When the lightning flashes and when the thunder rolls,
When the ocean crashes, in on my poor soul,
I have nowhere else to turn and nowhere else to go
But to the arms of Jesus, the only Savior that I know . . .
(CHORUS)

For a free download of the song "Trust," please visit WWW.TRUSTSTORY.ORG. As a bonus, you can also listen to and download two additional songs—"Earthly Point of View" and "Hope." This trilogy was written before, just after and several years after the tragedy that changed our lives forever. The music reflects our journey through grief and spiritual growth and will inspire you when life does not go as planned.

The Story Of "Trust"

"The LORD Will Provide" (Genesis 22:14).

Karen

The second week of February 2001 had been an extraordinarily busy week as my husband Phil and I fervently purged and packed in anticipation of our family's move across town. We loved our little home of ten years, but the newer lovely colonial-style house would be so much more suitable for our growing family: Our six-month-old baby Brett was currently in a tiny nursery off the noisy kitchen; our cheerful preschooler Zack had a niche that was previously half of our master bedroom; and our mature six-year-old Lindsay-Grace was in a room in the basement, apart from the rest of the family. Lindsay-Grace was especially excited about the move as she characteristically chronicled her joys in her journal and continually invited all her friends to visit her in our new home as soon as possible. Even though a different neighborhood would mean changing schools for Lindsay-Grace, we were not concerned because she was a motivated, excellent student who made friends easily. Our daughter was enthusiastic about life and her bright eyes and warm smile delighted all who knew her.

The Lazo family in front of their new home (2001)

Friday evening had finally come, and Phil and I looked forward to a quiet evening at home to watch TV and take a break from all our hard work getting ready for the move. It was the kids' bedtime, and we were determined to say goodnight as quickly as possible so we could relax and recharge for the next day of packing. However, Lindsay-Grace had other ideas. She used her charming wiles to convince her father to linger after "lights out" to listen to one of her favorite Bible story tapes with her. The selection that evening was the *Mr. Henry's Wild & Wacky Totally True Bible Stories*[i] rendition of Genesis 22:1–18 in which God tested Abraham's love for Him by asking this man to sacrifice his long-awaited and beloved son Isaac. Abraham trusted the Lord and believed that somehow He would provide a lamb for the sacrifice and that his son would be spared. With a knife in hand over his bound son, Abraham was about to strike a fatal blow when the angel of the Lord stopped him. God did, in fact, provide a sacrificial ram that was caught by its horns in a nearby thicket. The Lord honored Abraham's obedience and trust in Him by blessing all the nations of the earth through this patriarch and his offspring.

While Lindsay-Grace laughed at the one-liner

jokes and sound effects of this recorded rendition of the familiar Bible story, Phil was profoundly struck by the thought, "What if *I* were tested by God and had to choose between my earthly joys and comforts versus following the Lord (with the possibility of losing my child)?" At the conclusion of the story, he kissed Lindsay-Grace goodnight and, while holding back the tears, retreated to his music room and penned the words to a song he called "Trust." The song expressed the stinging question piercing the depths of his heart: What if he had to make a choice between God and his child, even if it meant being stripped of his hopes and dreams, causing his world to collapse and his days to be gripped with fear? He would, nevertheless, trust God.

Using his guitar, Phil soon poured these sentiments into music. However, "Trust" sat on the shelf for the next two years. In looking back, we can see that God gave my husband this song to prepare his heart for what was to come.

A few days after Phil wrote "Trust," our family made the big move across town. Baby Brett, fortunately, was not yet walking and still taking long naps, so he was not fazed by the change of scenery. Zack continued at his same pre-school, so it wasn't a hard adjustment for him either. Lindsay-Grace faced the most changes, but naturally blossomed in her new school and neighborhood and made many new friends. Throughout second grade, she became close with Rebecca, a sweet girl who lived right around the corner. The girls had a lot in common—both tall, thin, blond and smiley with a love of life. Unfortunately, they were classmates for only one year because Rebecca's family moved away the following summer. Although Lindsay-Grace was sad about Rebecca's move, she was thrilled to receive an invitation to her ninth birthday sleepover party on January 17–18, 2003.

Lindsay-Grace (2002)

Since the party was seventy-five miles away, some of Rebecca's friends from our town declined the invitation because they weren't comfortable spending the night that far from home. Reluctantly, one hesitant friend Kelsey did decide to attend and even had a practice sleepover the previous weekend at a local friend's house. When I called Kelsey's mom Anne to offer to drive her daughter to the party, Anne said that she wanted Kelsey to become comfortable with spending the night at someone else's home. Therefore, she was not planning to pick her daughter up in the middle of the night if Kelsey had second thoughts. However, second thoughts seemed far from Kelsey's mind when I picked her up that afternoon. Driving to the party, she and Lindsay-Grace had fun in the back seat of our minivan—talking, laughing, and doing what eight-year-old girls do.

In addition to Lindsay-Grace and Kelsey, our son Zack and his friend Ethan went along for the ride. Ethan was going to have a sleepover at our house and since the boys were friends with Rebecca's brother Zach, they thought it would be fun to visit with him again for a few minutes when we dropped off the girls.

That Friday evening, I drove the kids to the party in Keedysville, Maryland. An hour and a half away, Rebecca's house was more "out there" than I had imagined. The hilly roads through the forest to our destination were beautiful, but fading in the growing darkness by the minute. I wanted to make sure I could find my way out of their neck of the woods before it got too dark, so we only socialized a few minutes with Rebecca's family before heading home again. By then, Lindsay-Grace had become fully engaged in the party festivities. I managed to give her a quick peck on the cheek good-bye as she darted through the house with her friends.

Once on the road, in the back seat of our minivan, Zack and Ethan light-heartedly enjoyed their *Snow Dogs* DVD. In the front seat, I was not so carefree. I quickly realized that the directions to the house didn't work well in reverse because of some forks in the roads and the lack of visible street signs. I also discovered that a layer of ice had amassed on the hills. By God's grace, I eventually figured out my route but was not out of the woods yet (literally and figuratively). I drove up a hill and then to my shock, my car stopped going upwards and instead slid backwards through the darkness. A numb panic gripped my heart. I had two young kids in the vehicle and may be stuck in the middle of nowhere. I tried again to move the minivan forward, but after proceeding partway up the hill, we slipped back down to the bottom. I thought, "This time, I'll back up and get more of a running start." However, when I peered back through the darkness, I could now see the headlights of two other cars that had arrived, waiting to ascend the same slope. There was no room for me to get a running start. Fortunately, an angel on an ATV just happened to arrive and directed the other vehicles to slowly back up to give me more room. With a running start and fervent prayers—I finally succeeded! We got up and over the hill and were on our way home. Fortunately, the boys were engrossed in their movie and were unfazed by our harrowing circumstance. I, on the other hand, was rather haunted by the incident. Generally, I'm very optimistic and not easily rattled, but the scary drive out of that neighborhood just made me more acutely aware that, in the midst of my relatively trauma-free adulthood, things could actually go very wrong. In retrospect, the situation seemed to foreshadow something quite tragic that would happen the very next morning.

After a lively sleepover party, Rebecca and her friends woke and ate a hearty breakfast. Meanwhile,

Phil and I cheered for Zack at his early morning church-league basketball game. Our daughter's team, the Lady Buckeyes, was scheduled to play at 11:30, so the plan was for Rebecca's dad Doug to drop Lindsay-Grace off at the church in time for her pre-game warm-up and then drive Kelsey home.

Last picture taken of Lindsay-Grace,
at the party the evening before the accident (2003)

At 11:15 that Saturday morning, January 18, 2003, I waited in the lobby near the basketball game for Lindsay-Grace to arrive. It was a simple small foyer with a folding table, drinking fountain, trashcans, posted game schedules and directional signs. Not much to do there, except wait by the two sets of double glass doors and frequently scan the road and parking lot for the anticipated green Jeep Cherokee. The appointed meeting time came and went . . . then 11:30 . . . 11:45 . . . The game had already started. Where was he? Doug had never been to that church before, so perhaps he got lost? Maybe he forgot our arrangement and drove Kelsey home first? I called Rebecca's mother Bethany to see if she knew where they were. We called back and forth several times, hoping the other could provide an explanation or announce their arrival. The situation became increasingly worrisome when Bethany continually wasn't able to reach Doug by his cell phone or pager. One thing I learned was that Kelsey had gotten homesick in the middle of the night, so her mother had a change of heart and picked her up from the sleepover. So Doug would not have gone to Kelsey's house first. I also learned that Rebecca's eight-year-old sister Mandy had gone along for the ride to keep Lindsay-Grace company. (Rebecca, the birthday girl, couldn't join them because she still had guests at her home waiting to be picked up from the party.) Mandy didn't have anywhere else to go, so where could they be?

Finally, Bethany called me with the unfathomable news: "There's been an accident." She frantically told me that her husband Doug had been medevacked to the University of Maryland Shock Trauma Center in Baltimore, but no one would tell her where the girls were. I dropped to my knees and sunk my head into my crossed arms on the table. I just cried out in prayer, "Oh God—help us." The people nearby, who had become aware of our situation, gasped, gathered around me and dropped to their knees as well. After a few seconds, in shock, I rushed into the gym. Phil had been coaching Lindsay-Grace's team while continually looking to the doors every moment or two. Our eyes met, and the urgent, aghast look on my face gave him the message even before my words could be formed: "There's been an accident. We have to go."

"OH NO," Phil exclaimed. I could see the terror in his eyes.

Phil

All thoughts of the game disappeared from my mind as I grabbed my coat. An adrenaline rush of nervous energy came over me—the kind that often overtakes one when narrowly escaping an accident or injury. I turned to my sister Dede whose daughter played on Lindsay-Grace's team, and hastily asked her to take our two sons home with her while Karen and I went to find Lindsay-Grace.

We quickly left the church gym and got into our minivan. As we were about to drive away, we suddenly realized that we didn't know where we were going. I called 911 to ask where any recent accidents in the area had occurred. The dispatcher seemed hesitant to give us any information, but when I explained that our daughter was in the crash, they immediately transferred the call to the state police. After moments on hold, an officer came on the line. He, too, was hesitant to give us any information, but he indicated there was an accident on Interstate 70 Eastbound, near Route 97 in Howard County, Maryland.

During the somber ten-minute car ride to the crash site, Karen, as she so often does, was trying to look at all the possible positive outcomes. Despite the bitter cold, there was no precipitation, and the major highways seemed clear. Because of this (and the flashbacks of her troubles on the icy incline from the evening before), perhaps Doug's Jeep had just slipped over the edge of one of the steep hills into a ditch near his home. Also, the officer had not given us any medical transfer information about Lindsay-Grace and Mandy. So there was some hope that the girls were fine, and waiting for us by the side of the road. I sensed the worst but did not communicate that to Karen. After driving for a short while, I said, "We have to entertain the possibility that Lindsay-Grace could be dead." Karen acknowledged my thoughts. I then said, "This is where the rubber meets the road as far as our faith goes. This is where we see if we really believe what we say we believe."

Driving westbound on Route 70, we felt sick when we saw a horrific crash site on the eastbound side of the highway. Traffic was backed-up for miles behind it and emergency vehicles and television news trucks had already mobilized at the scene. I can't remember ever before seeing so many police, fire and rescue vehicles in one spot. Unable to cross the median, we drove past the site to the next exit and returned to the eastbound lane, driving slowly on the shoulder, working our way past the traffic jam. We parked the car on the side of the highway a few hundred yards away from the severed and smashed dark green Jeep Cherokee that had veered off the road at the curve and crashed into two trees. As if in a nightmare, we walked straight past a group of television reporters that had gathered on the scene. Karen asked them if they knew if anyone had been killed in the accident.

I quickly pulled my wife forward before they could answer: I did not want to hear from them if our daughter was dead.

As we continued toward the site of the one-car crash, a Maryland state trooper approached us with both his arms out in a "HALT" signal, stopping us in our tracks. He would not allow us to get any closer to the foreboding white sheets that were draped over and in front of the Jeep. We told the officer we needed to find out if our daughter was in that car and if she was still alive. He didn't know who we were, so he was very vague in his responses, giving us hardly any information. We told him our daughter was wearing a green and yellow basketball uniform and perhaps sweat pants. Upon hearing this, he finally said, "I've got two little girls up there and both of them are deceased."

My earlier suspicions had been confirmed but somehow it didn't seem real. We were stunned, not sure how to react or what to say. Amazingly, neither of us was hysterical. We didn't scream out or yell or break down on the grass crying. It was surreal, like a bad dream. We were simply in a state of shock.

The trooper offered us the back of his squad car to sit and absorb the enormity of what had happened.

It was a bitterly cold day and at first, the car, which had been left running, felt good. After a few minutes, however, it seemed unbearably hot. Karen and I prayed together for God's help then began to call our families and some close friends to tell them the heartbreaking news. Karen first called her mother in Virginia Beach, Virginia. Her mother's cheerfulness quickly turned to devastation as Karen, through her tears, told her the shocking news and asked her to come. Then, it was my turn to call my mother and father. Mom answered the phone. She already knew there had been an accident. I told her Lindsay-Grace was gone and she began screaming, "NO NO NO . . " I had to interrupt her and plead with her to not "freak out" on me. I needed her to calm down and, thankfully, she did.

I can't recall how long we were in that police car or at the scene of the crash but eventually we were told that our daughter would be taken to Howard County Hospital where we could identify the body. The policeman offered to drive us there, but we decided to drive ourselves so we could grieve privately. I tried to catch a glimpse of the wreck as we left the scene. It was difficult to discern the shape of the vehicle because of the damage. It almost looked like two cars

The Wrecked Car (after being moved from the accident location, 2003)

were involved because the Jeep had been ripped in two. Ironically, a green Jeep Cherokee was the first vehicle our newborn Lindsay-Grace rode in at the beginning of her life and the last she rode in at the end of her life.

On our way to the hospital, Karen and I were trying to process this catastrophe but we were remarkably calm. As we drove, the reality of our daughter never coming home again began to settle in, and I silently prayed that God would miraculously raise her from the dead. It was not an ultimatum for God with my agreeing to "attend church more" or "love my wife better," just a simple prayer asking God for the humanly impossible. I did not tell Karen that I had prayed this.

As we drove towards Howard County General Hospital in Columbia, Maryland, we realized that we didn't know exactly how to get there. We followed the blue hospital signs along the side of the road but had great difficulty finding it. It was rather strange dealing with such a normal life annoyance when our world had just been turned upside down. After about twenty minutes of driving around, we finally found the hospital and walked in through the emergency entrance. It was surreal for Karen to tell the receptionist that our daughter was going to be brought here DOA. How could those words be coming from my wife's mouth? What a distressed look on the nurse's face. She took us to a small room that reminded me of a hotel room, without the bed. There were chairs, a separate bathroom and a telephone available. We made some more calls to friends and wandered aimlessly around the room. Soon there was a knock on the door, and our good friend Doug Flather walked in. It was a great comfort to see Doug. He hugged us both. Shortly, more friends joined us: Chris Hill (a long-time, close friend),

Keith Matthews (our church's executive pastor) and Bryan Anderson (our church's worship pastor). Keith and Bryan had not known us very long as they had come to our church just about six months before this day. I was a little surprised to see them since we didn't know them well, but I was also very glad they came because we needed their comfort and support. To this day, we don't remember much of what they said to us, but we do deeply appreciate their presence and their tears, which meant more to us than words can express. We waited for quite some time for the emergency workers to bring Lindsay-Grace's body to the hospital from the accident scene. I'm not sure how long we waited, but it seemed like two hours. A compassionate nurse eventually came in to have us sign and date a stack of paperwork. Karen asked the date—January 18, 2003—and it occurred to us then how this date would be forever engraved on our hearts.

Finally, a hospital representative informed us that our daughter was ready, and we could go and see her. Suddenly, I was terrified. We knew she had a head injury, and I was afraid that it would be so severe that I wouldn't be able to handle it. I didn't want to see my precious daughter with a smashed head, and her gorgeous face destroyed. I told Karen and our friends that I was considering not going in to see Lindsay-Grace, so Chris offered to accompany my wife. The magnitude of what had happened over the past few hours was starting to settle over me. Karen went with Chris to see Lindsay-Grace while I stayed in the waiting room with Bryan, Keith and Doug.

Karen

After what seemed to be hours of waiting, I could finally see Lindsay-Grace. Accepting Chris' offer to go in with me, we walked down the hallway and entered a small room. I sobbed upon seeing our beautiful daughter lying face-up on the table in front of us. Lindsay-Grace didn't look as bad as I thought she would. From what was visible, her face was clear and looked mostly normal. She was cleaned-up and didn't have any obvious blood, cuts or bruises. However, she wasn't breathing and had no heartbeat. Her hands and face were ice-cold. Lindsay-Grace was wearing the sweat pants and basketball uniform I had packed for her the day before. Her tennis shoes were missing, lost in the violence of the crash. Her eyes were open and she had a blank look on her face. She didn't appear scared, which was a relief. The one thing that made her look injured was a white terry cloth hand towel that gently lay over the top right side of her head. I had to peek under the covering. What I saw haunts me to this day. Replacing the towel, I asked Chris to get Phil and tell him that, overall, her body wasn't too disturbing.

Phil

A few minutes later, Chris came back to the room where I was waiting. "I think you need to go see her," he said. I agreed. As we walked toward the viewing room, Chris very lovingly reminded me that this lifeless body I was about to see was not Lindsay-Grace anymore. She was now with God. Leaving Chris, I joined Karen to see our daughter for the last time. I kissed Lindsay-Grace and cried as I told her I loved her and I was sorry. In that moment and in the months and years ahead, my only real regret was that I was not able to protect her. A father needs to protect his family in many ways, including physically, but in this situation, I was unable. However, as I thought about it more, the fact that the accident was completely out of my control protected me from feeling guilty about her death.

I can't recall how long we were in that room. We sobbed on Lindsay-Grace's body, told her she did a great job in her life, gave her our last kisses on this side of heaven and said our good-byes.

Karen

After leaving the hospital, we drove to Phil's sister's house where the family had gathered and where Zack and Brett were waiting. I don't remember much about being there, but I do recall us sitting with Zack on his cousin's bed and telling him that Lindsay-Grace had died in the car crash. He cried and said he had thought she had died because he saw everyone looking very sad. In the true spirit of a six-year-old, his initial question was "Are we going to get rid of all her stuff?"

Brett, at the time, was two and a half. I don't remember us telling him directly about his sister's passing, but he soon kept declaring, "Lindsay-Grace is dead. Lindsay-Grace is dead." Because he was so young, he didn't grasp the enormous significance of what he was saying.

After a long, exhausting day, we finally drove back to our home. I cannot begin to express how strange (and quiet) it was without our vivacious eight-year-old there. Just inside our front door, her "Tweety Bird" denim school backpack, still with her classwork-stuffed "Friday folder," hung on the third hook in the foyer (where, incidentally, it stayed for almost six years until an exchange student moved in with us and his backpack took over that hook). Zack and his sister had shared a room and it was surreal to see her messy desk, art projects, Mary-Kate and Ashley Olsen posters, stuffed animals and toys—just how she had left them with the full intention of returning.

Despite feeling emotionally drained, I wanted to attend a prayer service for our family at church that evening. Phil needed to grieve privately and stayed home, so Elaine Hill, Chris' wife, drove me there and escorted me into the auditorium. The service was already underway when we arrived. I welcomed the opportunity to stand before all these friends, to tell them that Lindsay-Grace did not suffer and God was with us, giving us an abiding sense of calm amidst our tears. One of the first people I noticed was Lindsay-Grace's friend Kelsey who was sitting in the front row with her mother. Kelsey was the friend who should have also been in Doug's car that morning, but had gotten homesick and was driven home by her mother in the middle of the night. When it was time for people to gather into groups and pray, I joined Kelsey's circle first, praying for a special blessing on

Kelsey in the aftermath of what could have been a triple tragedy. It was bittersweet going around the auditorium, hugging everyone and praying with them that God would help us all in these dark days.

Back at home that night, we were exhausted but could hardly sleep. After going to bed, I got a call from the organ transplant coordinator who needed to go over information and authorization issues so a medical team could attempt to harvest our daughter's corneas and part of her heart. It felt like we were on that phone call for an hour, but it must have been less than that. We had requested from the beginning that Lindsay-Grace's organs be harvested, but, unfortunately, we learned later that there was too much damage and nothing could be used. This was a huge disappointment to us since we wanted a part of her to live on in someone else.

The next few tear-filled, sleep-deprived, phone-in-use days were a blur, but filled with unwavering consolation from family and those in our community. I hardly ate anything and lost six pounds in three days. Nevertheless, meals kept arriving at our home daily, along with cards, notes, relatives and friends. We felt so loved and supported. Gifts of service also meant a lot to us. People came to clean our house and eventually even painted and wallpapered. Our pastor at the time, Brian McLaren, went above and beyond any call of duty. He guided us through making arrangements with the funeral home, sent us many encouraging emails and came to our home often, spending hours hashing through whatever was on our minds:

"Do you think she had time to be scared?"

"Is she in heaven right now, even though she hadn't yet been baptized?"

"How do I deal with haunting mental images of her head injury?"

Phil

We were in deep pain, but overall, we had an abiding sense of peace and calm that could only come from God. We somehow felt protected and sheltered. We weren't denying what was going on but incredibly, we felt safe . . . at peace. The Bible says, "the peace of God, which transcends all understanding, will guard your hearts and your minds in Christ Jesus" (Philippians 4:7). I grew up in a Christian home and attended church my whole life. I had heard this verse many, many times. Now, I truly knew what it meant. We were being guarded by God's peace. Karen and

I had been Christians for a long time and although the love for our daughter and two sons had always been intensely deep, our children had never been the center of our universe or the foundation of our lives. That place of honor belonged (and still belongs) only to God, "my rock, my fortress and my deliverer . . . in whom I take refuge" (Psalm 18:2). Therefore, we felt we could relate to the Apostle Paul when he wrote in 2 Corinthians 4:8–9—"We are hard-pressed on every side, but not crushed; perplexed, but not in despair . . . struck down, but not destroyed."

Karen

On the Thursday morning after the accident, Phil, Zack, Brett and I arrived early to Lindsay-Grace's "Celebration of Life" service. Having parked on the side of our church, we made a quick beeline into the worship center so we could have some private moments with our daughter before facing everyone. She was in a closed casket, of course, because of her head injury. Although we couldn't touch Lindsay-Grace, being near her body was a consolation. We were also comforted by all the special things already put in place by faithful friends and family members: Lindsay-Grace's simple creamy white coffin was topped with her favorite teddy bears and stuffed dog, next to an arrangement of pink roses and purple heather. The coffin sat under a canopy arch of blue and white balloons topped with a silver balloon shaped like a heart. There was a slideshow of fifty pictures of our happy girl being projected on big screens while her favorite songs filled the auditorium. Lots of food was being prepared in the side rooms. In addition, there were baskets with 250 goody bags for her friends who were expected to attend. Each bag included a "Fruit by the Foot" snack (her favorite), a "gospel bead" backpack clip and a wallet-sized photo of Lindsay-Grace mounted on a lovely flowered card printed with her name and the Bible verse John 3:16.[ii] The culmination of efforts of countless friends and family meant so much to us. Although we cried, we were at peace.

Walking into the church foyer, we were greeted by so many people. They were all there to celebrate the wonderful life, yet grieve the profound loss, of Lindsay-Grace. Phil and I were astonished by the distance many had come and by the presence of people with whom we'd lost contact. (How did they hear our news?) It was amazing to see dear ones from all aspects of our lives—college, single days, work, present and former neighborhoods—all together in one place. We were stunned as close to 650 people filed into the auditorium. All the seats were eventually filled, so excess people stood along the back and side walls. The overflow crowd sat in the foyer, with access to the television monitors showing the service.

After introductory words of welcome, the praise band led us in worship with songs about the Lord's goodness, grace and love. Some may think that songs such as "Great is Thy Faithfulness" and "Shout to the Lord" would be out of place at a child's memorial service, but these and other songs articulated our deepest awareness that the Lord was still on His throne, no matter what. Initially, everyone sat and sang, but soon, most were standing and singing in genuine worship. In the weeks that followed, many people told us that they had never before experienced the presence of God as they did that morning in the service.

After prayers and Scripture reading, Lindsay-Grace's eulogy was presented as an "open mic" opportunity for whoever wanted to participate. Many classmates of Lindsay-Grace had come to the service, and it meant so much to us to hear them say how much they loved their friend and what they remembered about her. It touched my heart to hear how many of them considered Lindsay-Grace to be their best friend because she made them feel so special. We chuckled and wept as wave after wave of relatives, friends and teachers came forward to share their stories and sentiments.

We were so thankful to have our dear friend and pastor, Brian, give the message. He choked up as he shared how he heard our horrible news, yet offered inspiration in sharing the Biblical story of Jairus' twelve-year-old dead daughter whom Jesus brought back to life.[iii] The story seemed to be in stark, ironic contrast to our story because our daughter was *not* given back to her parents as Jairus' daughter had been. However, Brian encouraged us to look at the story again: Among other points, he reminded us that Lindsay-Grace was indeed "awakened" to hear Jesus say, "Little girl, arise" (just as in the story), but Phil and I are seeing our child's new life with spiritual eyes instead of our earthly eyes. This is a reality. She truly is alive. Also, Brian explained how this account is a window into the heart of God: If one wants to understand the way God feels about him, he can go to the deepest love one can find anywhere—that is the love a parent has for his child (as in the story and with us). In God's eyes, we too are precious, beloved, irreplaceable and cherished. Having this knowledge transforms our hearts and causes comfort to flow into all our sadness. It was inspirational for us to open our hearts wider to receive all that God wants to give to us now and forever.

Phil and I had the opportunity to share about our daughter. I spoke composedly, painting a portrait of a lively youngster who was not perfect, but more poignantly, a real child. Lindsay-Grace peeled her nails, threw her clothes into the laundry after wearing them for twenty minutes, forgot her chores and bossed around her younger brother. Nevertheless, she was bright, mature beyond her years, intelligent, enthusiastic and kind. She loved to be with her friends; she loved to read, write, learn and perform. I explained that although Lindsay-Grace was my daughter, she was also like a buddy to me. We had a great relationship, and I kept forgetting that she wasn't with us anymore. I just couldn't imagine life without her. Nevertheless, I articulated how faith had sustained us: "We've been so heart-broken and have cried and cried, but God has given us such a river of peace. Overall, deep inside, we really are okay. We have a weird peace about this and a sense of anticipation about the lives that are going to be changed because of our girl."

Phil was up next. He talked about one of his favorite memories with Lindsay-Grace—the time they went sledding in the breath-taking snowy woods. My husband read a sentimental poem[iv] that had been given to him as well. Earlier that week, we realized the amazing relevance of Phil's song to our situation. So after Phil shared his memories, he played the pre-recorded "Trust" song while showing a slide show presentation featuring the song lyrics and pictures of Lindsay-Grace and him together.

Within a week, many people were requesting a copy of the "Trust" song, so Phil and his band Northbound collaborated on a better recording of it and produced a CD. It featured a double-fold jacket cover that explained the story behind the song and encouraged people to trust their lives to God *before* the storms of life come their way. We gave a CD to whoever asked for one and had them available in a rack in our church's foyer. Also, in subsequent years, when my husband and I were invited to share our story (in churches, at seminars, on retreats or as part of Phil's Northbound band concerts), we had them available afterwards for anyone who wanted one.

The Original Cover of our "Trust" CD (2003)

Through having the opportunities to share our story publicly, Phil and I were astonished to go through one thousand of the "Trust" CDs in the first two weeks, a second thousand in the next nine months, a third thousand in the next eighteen months and a fourth thousand in the couple years after that! As of 2014, we are going through our fifth thousand. We did not sell the discs, but nevertheless, people gave us donations. The financial gifts were enough to fund the construction of the "Lindsay-Grace Lazo Community Playground" on our church's property and to also start and maintain a relief program (in conjunction with World Relief) for poverty-stricken children in Sierra Leone, Africa. Extra contributions were used to defray the cost of additional CDs so they could continue to be given away for free.

As the rawness of our tragedy subsided over the years, so did the donations. However, it was interesting how the Lord provided the funds to pay for more orders of discs. In 2005, our family had the opportunity to travel to the UK to visit some dear friends and share our story at their church. Before our trip, we needed to order another thousand of the "Trust" CDs so we could have them available for our speaking engagement in England. Even though purchasing them would put a strain on our bank account, we ordered them anyway, trusting God for the finances to pay our next credit card bill. On the day of our trip, we waited two hours in the British Airways check-in line. Just when we got to the front of the line, an agent stepped out from a back room and announced that the flight was overbooked. Anyone who was willing to wait for the next flight would be paid $400 per person in cash! Our family of four accepted the offer and walked out of there with a stack of cash, $92 in meal vouchers and a free night in a nearby five-star hotel. We ended up on a better flight (i.e. not red-eye) early the next day, spoke at a church the following morning and were amazed by the generous financial gifts we were given. Between these donations and the airline money, the price of the next thousand CDs was covered!

When we look at the piece of notebook paper on which "Trust" was written so many years ago, we are amazed how TRUST (in God, that is!) has been a recurring theme in our lives ever since that horrible January morning. As we absorbed the trauma of Lindsay-Grace's death into our lives, God, by His grace, did many amazing things and taught us so much. We hesitated to write this book because we did not want to imply that the Lord would always intervene in obvious ways in tragedies as He did with us. God's mysterious ways are often not our ways[v], but He promises to never leave or forsake us[vi], even if we can't sense His presence. We also don't want this book to be a manual on how to best deal with calamities, because people are in different places in their journeys with God and there is no single correct way for everyone to process grief and find hope when life does not go as planned. However, as I was reminded just this morning in my Bible study, "let your light shine before others, that they may see your good deeds and glorify your Father in heaven."[vii] We need to tell this story to share how powerful, caring and personal our God is. Also, in hopes of providing encouragement to those struggling, we are sharing some of the most helpful nuggets of wisdom that we discovered in our journey through grief and trials.

Trusting God for Preparation

"Before they call, I will answer;
while they are still speaking, I will hear" (Isaiah 65:24).

The most crucial element of our preparedness for this tragedy was that both of us already had a relationship with God before January 18, 2003. Even though our quiet testimonies of how we came to faith aren't the thrilling, gripping tales that others may be able to share, they are no less significant.

Phil

I grew up in a home where Jesus was honored and taught, and we regularly attended a church where it was easy to learn about God. I'm thankful that I had this environment in which to grow up. It helped foster a natural love of the Lord. As a young boy, I learned that Jesus died on the cross to take the punishment for our sins and that I could accept this gift and be in a relationship with Him. I believed in Jesus and asked Him to be my Savior, but it wasn't until I was about nineteen, that I let Christ be the leader of every part of my life. This was due largely in part to the growth opportunities offered to me in my vibrant youth group at McLean Bible Church in McLean, Virginia. I have never regretted my decision to ask Jesus to be my Lord and, as a result, have never been the same. I have peace in knowing that my sins are forgiven and that God is in control of everything that will ever happen. The promise of heaven that Jesus offers is exciting, but the adventure of journeying through this life with Him at my side also brings me unspeakable joy. An understanding that God deeply loves me permeates my life. Without Jesus, life simply would not be as much fun, and it would be a lot more stressful.

Karen

While I was growing up, most weeks, our family went to church where I learned about God. I remember, as a young child, sitting in my bathtub and, while reflecting on my Sunday school lesson, asking Jesus to be part of my life and thanking Him for taking the punishment for my sins. Years later, in high school, I was walking home from the bus stop on a bright sunny day and just felt compelled to take God more seriously on days other than just Sunday. So, I started regularly reading my Bible, praying and getting involved with the church youth group. That summer, our group went on a work mission trip to Mexico and, being so inspired by the Christians I met during that adventure, I decided to follow Jesus more whole-heartedly. My life has never been the same; my relationship with God brings me a deep joy, peace and hope, no matter what happens.

Phil

I'm not saying Karen's and my faith in God was perfect—far from it. However, we had been journeying with the Lord for many years by the time our daughter passed away and, we found out in the weeks after the accident, that God had long-been preparing us for what was to come. For example, our family was enveloped in prayer even before we knew we needed it. The following three stories illustrate how the Lord was working:

Tori, one of Lindsay-Grace's closest friends from

church, was having frequent dreams that someone close to her was going to die. On some mornings, she would wake up and announce that she didn't have the dream that previous night, but she still had the feeling that someone close was going to die. Her family consequently often prayed for the situation— not knowing they were praying for us. Tori had the dream two days before the crash, and when she heard the news that Lindsay-Grace had passed away, she told her mom that Lindsay-Grace was the one whom her visions concerned. Tori never had that dream again.

The following is an excerpt from a letter we received from a friend from church several weeks after the accident. We had known this woman for about ten years—she is a quiet, God-loving, down-to-earth mother, not someone who would make up such an incredible tale:

> *I have a story to share with you that, to be quite honest, I was not going to share with anyone because it is a bit on the freaky side—But as you all were speaking on Sunday, God spoke quietly to my heart to share it with you both. I hope and pray that it will bring some encouragement to you. Sometime in late December or early January,*

one of the last times I saw Lindsay-Grace alive, I was near the second-grade classroom at church. When I looked at Lindsay-Grace, I had the strange sensation that I was almost looking through her— like she was transparent or something. This has happened to me exactly once before in my life— when I saw a friend from college several years before he passed away from cancer. I thought this is really odd—she is a healthy, happy little girl. What is going on??? As I turned to walk away, my heart suddenly felt very sad, and I heard a voice in my mind almost like an echo . . . "How will they ever live without her?" By this time, I was thinking that I was totally loopy. I had forgotten this incident until at the memorial service, Karen, you said something like . . . "I don't know how we are going to live without her." I began questioning the Lord in prayer: "Why, why did You give me— whatever You want to call this?" And very quietly, the Lord placed these words in my heart, "What was your response?" Well (after the incident), after thinking I was totally crazy and before dismissing it as some freaky, weird thought, I did what I often do when things don't make sense to me . . . I prayed. I prayed for your family, I prayed for Lindsay-Grace. I can't remember what I prayed but you see, Karen and Phil, God was calling people to lift up your family in prayer even before anything happened.

Another incident of prayers for us involved one of Lindsay-Grace's third-grade teachers, Mrs. Oldham. She told us that whenever she and her husband would see an accident or an ambulance, as they would drive along, they would send up a prayer for those involved. On the morning of January 18, she and her husband were driving on I-70 and they saw, at the edge of the woods, the crashed car in which Lindsay-Grace had been riding. For the first time ever, they felt compelled to pull their car over to the side of the road by the accident and pray for the whole situation. Mrs. Oldham had no idea at the time that she was praying for the family of one of her very own students.

Obviously, God was leading people to pray for us, so that when we heard the horrible news, our hearts and spirits were more prepared to accept it.

How can you be in a relationship with a God who promises to prepare you for whatever storms may come your way? If you choose, you may read the epilogue at the end of this book that tells you how.

Trusting God for Comfort

"The righteous cry out, and the LORD hears them;
he delivers them from all their troubles.
The LORD is close to the brokenhearted
and saves those who are crushed in spirit" (Psalm 34:17–18).

Even though we grieved heavily and cried thousands of tears, deep in our hearts, we experienced comfort. We clung to God's promises through the Scriptures that brought us deep peace, assurance that our suffering would not go on forever and joy that Lindsay-Grace is alive with God in heaven. The following are some examples of how God comforted us in those early weeks after Lindsay-Grace's passing.

Karen

One way that the Lord consoled me in my grief was through a dream. It was so clear and real. I saw Lindsay-Grace in the distance walking toward me and was concerned that she was coming such a long way all by herself without a grown-up. As she got closer, I was overwhelmed by the sensation that she was completely safe and totally enveloped by the feeling that she was my girl but not *really* my girl—she belonged to her Creator who lent her to us for eight years. Lindsay-Grace looked gorgeous, especially her brown eyes which were shining and absolutely beautiful. Her hair was so clean and shiny with a bit of wave and tangle-free for the first time ever. She leaned into me with her characteristic brief sideways hug, but was anxious to continue walking, go through a turnstile and join some other people going somewhere. She was nonchalant about confidently going on ahead of me (as she always had been in life here on earth), but when I tried to follow, I couldn't get through the turnstile at this place because I was told I hadn't yet been given my token for admittance. I would have to wait for an indefinite amount of time before being able to catch up with her. Remarkably, I felt okay about that. What a peaceful and encouraging dream this was. It was fantastic to see Lindsay-Grace again, and I truly experienced the realization that she is safe, gorgeous, well cared for, cherished and totally fine with going on ahead of me.

Phil

Another way God brought us comfort was through an email from an acquaintance, Deana Ruhl, a friend of my sister. It was amazing that this came to us less than a month after the accident, and on the very day that our pastor Brian and we had discussed for hours Biblical evidence that showed Lindsay-Grace was actually alive *now* with Jesus. This conversation helped us be more secure with this belief, but when this poem arrived, it encouraged us even more.

> *Hi guys—During my prayer time today, these words TOTALLY came to me from the Lord. I sat down at the computer and wrote this in less than five minutes because I felt the Lord speaking through me (not because I am some poet or something). I felt that the Lord wanted me to send this to you. We love you, Deana and family*

"Guess What, Mommy and Daddy?"

Dedicated to Phil & Karen in special memory
of Lindsay-Grace Lazo

Heaven is great,
Just like you said.
I don't cry at all,
And I don't have to go to bed!

The streets made of gold
Are shiny and new!
They shine from Jesus' love
And I feel brand new!

You must miss me so,
The loss you can't hack;
But if for some reassurance,
I'm so happy, I don't want to come back!

Wonderful people are here—
You would not believe!
I am so content here
So for me, do not grieve.

Does it soften the blow
To know that I am safe?
To know that I am comforted,
That I now truly know God's grace?

My middle name Grace,
You knew God would show.
Let my eight years on earth
Be precious and grow.

Let the growth be a witness
Of your love for God too.
I will be so excited
As new believers to heaven come through.

I will eagerly listen as they tell me,
"Your Mommy and Daddy told me your story,
And because of their faith,
I am now here in Glory!"

Heaven is great,
Just like you said!
You were right for teaching me
From the Bible you read!

I am writing to tell you
That what you taught me is true!
Please remind others
That Jesus loves me and you.

These verses cut us right to the heart because they addressed so many of the issues that were concerning us. This poem was a gift from God confirming that Lindsay-Grace is alive, content, happy and safe in heaven with Him. It also reflected the fact that our daughter always had an uncanny interest in heaven—we even have video of her talking about it when she was about six years old, and we have pictures that she drew of heaven when she was even younger. Also, we were amazed to learn that this poem flowed from an author who hardly knew our family and had seldom, if ever, written poetry before. However, Lindsay-Grace did write poetry, and this style and meter was the same type that she used when she wrote her verses. In fact, the day before Lindsay-Grace's passing, her teacher submitted a poetry book our daughter had written into the county "Write-a-Book" competition. In the spring after the car accident, we learned Lindsay-Grace's book won first place in the poetry division!

We are not sure how to explain Deana's poem. The Bible often speaks of "signs and wonders"—events that happen that can't fully be explained in human terms—so this must be one of those wonders. However, we like to imagine that Jesus allowed

Lindsay-Grace to write this poem and then He gave it to this acquaintance to deliver it to us. Who knows? It is truly a mystery, but I do know that receiving this email was a tremendous encouragement to us.

Karen

A third example of how God encouraged us evolved around a Biblical story recounted three times in the New Testament. It tells of Jesus bringing back to life the deceased daughter of a man named Jairus. That narrative became relevant to us three times that first week. It was amazing how this story kept surfacing.

On the Friday afternoon before the accident, Lindsay-Grace and her brother Zack came home from school, bursting with excitement, ready for their fun weekend with friends and basketball games. Because we needed to leave for Rebecca's sleepover party in an hour, we decided to do our family devotions early that day. We had been working through the *Jesus* film,[viii] watching a few minutes every day and then talking about the story. The clip of the day was about Jairus' daughter from Luke 8. The *Scooby Doo* show followed at 3:00, then at 3:30, Lindsay-Grace left our home for the last time and we drove to the sleepover.

Luke 8:40-42 and 49-56

Now when Jesus returned, a crowd welcomed him, for they were all expecting him. Then a man named Jairus, a synagogue leader, came and fell at Jesus' feet, pleading with him to come to his house because his only daughter, a girl of about twelve, was dying.

As Jesus was on his way, the crowds almost crushed him. . . .

While Jesus was still speaking, someone came from the house of Jairus, the synagogue leader. "Your daughter is dead," he said. "Don't bother the teacher anymore."

Hearing this, Jesus said to Jairus, "Don't be afraid; just believe, and she will be healed."

When he arrived at the house of Jairus, he did not let anyone go in with him except Peter, John and James, and the child's father and mother. Meanwhile, all the people were wailing and mourning for her. "Stop wailing," Jesus said. "She is not dead but asleep."

They laughed at him, knowing that she was dead. But he took her by the hand and said, "My child, get up!"* Her spirit returned, and at once she stood up. Then Jesus told them to give her something to eat. Her parents were astonished, but he ordered them not to tell anyone what had happened.

*or in Aramaic, *"Talitha Koum" which means, "Little girl, arise."*

Little did I realize the significance that story about Jairus' daughter would have in our lives. At 10:45 the next morning, Lindsay-Grace was gone. The following morning, our pastor, Brian, who had been out of cell phone range on Saturday, was arriving at a California airport when he heard our tragic news. Amidst his tears, as he checked his bags, he sensed the words in his spirit, "Little girl, arise." As he sat in the plane flying back to Maryland, he studied the context of these words Jesus spoke in the story of Jairus' daughter. Without realizing the significance this passage of Scripture had to us, he ended up using it as the basis of his message at Lindsay-Grace's memorial service. Through this story, God drew hundreds of people closer to Him that morning.

The story of Jairus' daughter resurfaced a few days later as well. Phil and I attended a Super Bowl party given in our honor on the Sunday after the "Celebration of Life" service. It was great to not only relax with friends in front of the televised football game, but also to hear stories of wonderful things that had been happening in people's lives the previous days. However, it was a school night, so I went home at halftime to put our sons Zack and Brett to bed while Phil stayed at the gathering to watch the end of the game.

After getting the boys settled at home, I checked my emails. Every day that week, I had received emails from people coming to faith, reconciling with their children, deciding to go back to church, etc. These meant the world to me and had been helping me through my grief. However, when I logged on to my account, for the first time that week, there were no new emails about changed lives. There were no stories about Lindsay-Grace or words of encouragement from friends promising to pray for us. Also, I noticed for the first time that some of the memorial flower arrangements were starting to die. Suddenly, an unfamiliar voice in my spirit taunted me expressing, *"Lindsay-Grace's story is over. That's it. It's been an encouraging week spiritually for everyone, but now everyone is going to get back to the way they were before."* I collapsed into our recliner and cried and cried and cried. "Please, Lord, I need another story . . ." When I finally amassed the strength to climb the stairs and collapse in bed, I just wanted to fall into a deep slumber and wake up and have this all be a bad dream. I had never felt so despondent in my life.

When Phil got home an hour later, we cried out in prayer to the Lord, begging for encouragement for our broken hearts. Within three minutes of our prayer, the phone rang—at 11:30 at night. Who would have the nerve to call *anyone* at that hour, let alone a grieving family? It was Bonnie, our former neighbor and babysitter, calling from New Jersey. She apologized for calling so late but said she sensed the urgency to tell us something that had just happened: Bonnie had gone to bed, couldn't sleep and, uncharacteristically, got out of bed and checked her email. The previous day, Bonnie had signed-up to receive online daily Bible devotionals. Amazingly, the story that was emailed to her so late that night was the one about Jesus raising Jairus' daughter from the dead. Bonnie was shocked that she happened to receive that story because she remembered it was the context of the message during Lindsay-Grace's memorial service.

When Bonnie read the email devotional, Jesus' words to the girl's parents, "Don't be afraid, just believe," strongly stood out to her. Bonnie felt strongly that she had to call me to tell me those words. Those words cut straight to our broken hearts: We *were* afraid—afraid of thinking how dark, sad and unsatisfying our lives might be without our daughter. However, our Lord was telling us *not* to be afraid, but just to believe. He assured us that night that He was still in control.

Bonnie went on to say the memorial service had a profound impact on her and her new husband. They had decided during the long drive home that they wanted to find a church and have God be a part of their lives. This young woman has always held a special place in my heart, so hearing her intentions was a dream-come-true for me because I had been concerned about the possibly of her falling away from her childhood faith. We were deeply comforted by Bonnie's call and I fell asleep with a smile on my face that night. One more story had come my way, just when I needed it the most.

Many people have asked how our sons have been, since losing their sister. We have seen that God has been faithful in comforting them as well. It has helped to keep the lines of communication open with them, be vulnerable enough to cry in front of them and to continually share how the Lord is bringing good out of the tragedy.

We did have some initial concerns about Zack, our older son. Because he didn't show a lot of emotion and continued to be fairly optimistic as he normally was, I was concerned that perhaps he was suppressing his emotions too much. He did climb in bed with us the first couple nights after the accident, saying, "I want Lindsay-Grace alive again." Zack expressed in his prayers the hope that the rest of us wouldn't die too. He also struggled with the nagging question, "Why didn't she just jump out of the car? That's what *I* would have done." However, after the first few days, Zack just seemed to be relatively unfazed. So, I consulted with a Christian pediatric psychologist who told me that it was not out of the realm of normalcy for a six-year-old to have a childlike faith in understanding his sister is in heaven, even more so than adults. When our son was young, he had birthmarks on his left shoulder that looked like fingerprints. Although they have faded with time, we still believe that Someone has had His hand on Zack through all of this.

Brett, too, weathered the storm of his sister's passing relatively well. Because he was only two and a half, his young mind just could not fully grasp the enormity of the situation. Lindsay-Grace had always doted on her baby brother, playing with him and reading to him, so Brett definitely missed her and we heard him calling for her from his bed the first few mornings after the accident. However, Brett never cried much about the loss when he was little. It's interesting to note, that as the years went on, Brett would mention specific memories of Lindsay-Grace and himself that no one else had told him, such as her spinning the bumble bee-shaped fan pull above the kitchen table to make it look like the bee was going to attack. He also described his sister bouncing him on her back as she carried him to the house from our back yard trampoline. In addition, Brett has had some very vivid dreams and early-morning visions over the years of his sister waving to him (in his room or outside) and saying, "Hey, Brett!" Although he was too young to remember a lot about his sister, these personal memories and experiences have been a great gift for him.

God, by His mercy, did much to soften our pain. People often ask us what we did to find comfort in the aftermath of our loss. Aside from pouring our hearts out to God, it was extremely helpful for us to seek godly counsel from wise individuals who helped us reframe our perspective on our grief. We learned to never underestimate the value of seeking consultation with professional grief counselors or clergy. Our pastor Brian spent many hours with us in those early months after the accident, giving us countless nuggets of wisdom. For example, we were grieving the fact that Lindsay-Grace would miss so much in this life. Brian reminded us that although she's not going to sled down a snowy hill, graduate from college, get married, visit Hawaii, etc.—all the feelings associated with these activities—thrills, joy, beauty, peace, acceptance, laughter, accomplishment and love—she already has in a larger capacity and will have forever. After all, her Lord didn't create her for eight years— He created her for eternity.

Another thing that I struggled with was the haunting images of Lindsay-Grace's head trauma in the hospital. This email from Brian was one that helped me so much and has application for anyone grappling with negative memories:

> *Karen—thanks for your note. This sounds like something worth talking about in person. How about I come by on Friday this week, maybe 11 a.m.? In the meantime, here's what I'd recommend. If the picture in your mind from the hospital seems oppressive, like it's crowding in on your thoughts against your will and disturbing you, try this three-step process.*

1. In prayer, say something like this to God: "Lord, this image in my mind is reminding me that my loss is real. Help me to accept this and cope with it and process it with your help. It's so hard to accept and believe. It's so sad. God I share my sadness with you. Please comfort me!"

2. Then, consciously try to bring another image to your mind—the picture of her sledding with Phil, or some other good memory. In prayer, say something like this to God: "God, thank you for these good memories with my daughter. Thank you for the gift of her life. Thank you for all the good days and good times we shared."

3. Then, turn to the future in prayer: "God, I look forward to my future, even though I have experienced this crushing loss, and I ask you to give me strength for the tasks of today. Help me specifically to . . . " and then ask for help with "the next right things" you need to do. (Remember how we talked about the value of daily duties and responsibilities?)

Let me know if these three steps help you . . .

*accepting the memory from the hospital, replacing
it with another memory, and looking ahead . . . all
in a spirit of prayer.*

With you and Phil in spirit—Brian

Another good suggestion for our comfort was to plan circumstances to "look forward to." Brian encouraged Phil and me to take a trip together without the boys. We visited the theme parks in Orlando, Florida that greatly lifted our spirits. In the months after our loss, it was therapeutic for us to do some home improvement projects that we had long wanted to do, like paint some rooms, rearrange our bedroom and buy a new couch. These accomplishments truly did bring us some happiness.

In addition to talking with our pastor, we discovered the value of talking with people further down the road in their grief and others who have dealt with similar circumstances. It would be ideal to reach out to a friend or trusted acquaintance. Otherwise, an Internet search will often reveal support networks with live and/or virtual chapters in which one can connect with others who have journeyed similar paths. In my case, a year after Lindsay-Grace's passing,

God unexpectedly brought an individual into my life who was a great inspiration to me. While attending a Children's Ministry Conference in San Diego, California, I was on my way to a workshop that I had selected. As I was passing the doorway of a different workshop, I suddenly sensed the urgency to go into this one instead. Having learned to heed this still, small voice, I went in there, with just a quick glance at the room assignment sign to see what the workshop session was about. The chairs were arranged in a big semi-circle around the room, and I sat in the last empty seat available, which just happened to be behind the presenter.

The leader of the workshop was Jana Alayra, a nationally renowned musician and conference speaker. Her session featured new songs and movements for kids' worship. Even though I had originally decided not to participate in any music workshops at this conference, I gleaned some fantastic ideas from that seminar, and was newly inspired in my role as a kids' worship leader at church.

In the last part of the class, Jana shared her personal story. I was astonished to hear that her young daughter was killed in an automobile accident a few years earlier. It was quite inspiring to see this smiling, joyful woman who was further down the road after enduring a similar tragedy. She continued to love God and serve Him enthusiastically despite her profound loss.

Since my seat was right behind her, I was able to jump up at the end of the session and speak with her briefly before her crowd of fans swarmed around her. I was weeping and told her how I initially didn't plan to be in her workshop but God *forced* me into the room. This conversation was the beginning of an inspirational friendship. Although she was based in California, we prayed for each other and corresponded periodically via email. We even were able to meet again the following spring when she was performing on the East Coast. In getting to know her, I felt empowered and comforted that I too would be joyful again and be able to enthusiastically serve God.

Phil

In addition to getting encouragement from others, we have gained countless wise insights and consolation through books we have read. My favorite author is John Eldredge, who has written several thought-provoking books for Christians in general and men in particular. These have applications for anyone who wants to trust God more fully for a meaningful life. In the years after Lindsay-Grace died, I read the books *Wild At Heart, Waking The Dead, The Way of the Wild Heart* (later titled *Fathered by God*), *Desire* and *Walking with God*. An extraordinary truth Eldredge communicated was that God cherishes me in ways I had never fully understood. I believed and trusted that Jesus loved me and had died on the cross to take the punishment for my sins. However, I gained a deeper understanding that I was loved by God more immensely than I had realized and that He desires to journey with me through each phase of life and in every good and bad moment. I also learned that the core of my being, my heart, has been made good by Jesus' sacrifice and that I have a role to play in what the Lord is doing here on earth. My story can be used to bring Him glory. I deeply wanted this. He wants more from me than mere duty and obligation, even though I am happy to serve Him. He desires intimacy. This knowledge, in turn, makes me love Him more. These lessons learned brought hope and comfort and also reshaped the way I viewed my life.

Karen

One of the books that meant the most to us was Nancy Guthrie's *Holding on to Hope*. (I mention insights from her writing throughout this memoir.) Another book that encouraged us a lot was *Brokenness: How God Redeems Pain and Suffering*, written by our former pastor Lon Solomon. This has insights for people who are not only grieving the loss of a loved one, but also those who grieve the loss of a dream. It made us realize that down through history, the Lord has done mighty things through His people who suffered. In fact, think about any person in the Bible who was used by God in powerful ways. Whoever one may choose—for example, Jesus, Moses, Abraham, Mary, David, Isaiah, Jacob, Joseph, Paul— each of these people was chosen for tremendous suffering. Their stories provided us with perspective, reminding us that God's children do not experience meaningless suffering. The Lord allows it into our lives for a purpose. Pastor Solomon articulates this well:

> *You and I as followers of Christ, cannot and will not see God's anointing and power manifested through us until brokenness becomes a reality in our lives. And the more broken we are, the more of God's anointing and power we will experience.*[ix]

No one regrets being broken, because on the other side of brokenness lies a new intimacy with God and new power to serve Him. However, no one would dare say it was easy or that they ever wanted to go through it again.[x]

About a year and a half after Lindsay-Grace's death, our family finally had the emotional strength to use a butterfly set that she had received on her last birthday. This gift included a pop-up pavilion that came with a certificate for caterpillars (that we ordered and received through the mail). Following the instructions, we watched in amazement over the next couple weeks as the caterpillars ate their food and formed their chrysalises. As we watched them struggle to break free of their hard-shelled pupae, it was very tempting to help them open their cases. If we just intervened a little bit, wouldn't they appreciate it? After all, wouldn't this help them reach their desired state more quickly? On the contrary, if we had helped them break out of their chrysalises, our tiny pets would have died. They needed to strain and struggle in order to develop strength and survive. After they emerged as painted lady butterflies, they were soon able to fly. What a life lesson this was for us: As with the Biblical heroes of faith, God lets struggle to enable us to soar. Without strain, there i no strength.

In retrospect, I can see that God had already made me stronger to handle Lindsay-Grace's passing because of losses I suffered earlier in life. As an example, one dark, foggy evening when I was in third grade, my father was killed in a plane crash. It's ironic that I lost a parent when I was a child of eight and I lost a child of eight when I was a parent. My mother reared my two brothers and me well and remained a widow for thirty-one years until she remarried later in life. Other major heartbreaks were more recent in my life: Despite whole-heartedly begging God for mercy, I miscarried a baby halfway through my first pregnancy. A couple years later, I lost Zack's twin early in my third pregnancy.

Another insight about finding comfort from grief or disappointment was articulated well in Jerry Sittser's book *A Grace Disguised*. The author describes a dream he had after the horrific loss of three family members in an automobile accident:

I dreamed of a setting sun. I was frantically running west, trying desperately to catch it and remain in its fiery warmth and light. But I was losing the race. The sun was beating me to the horizon and was soon gone. I suddenly found myself in the twilight. Exhausted, I stopped running and glanced back with foreboding over my shoulder to the east. I saw a vast darkness closing in on me. I was terrified by that darkness. I wanted to keep running after the sun, though I knew that it was futile, for it had already proven itself faster than I was. So, I lost all hope, collapsed to the ground, and fell into despair. I thought at that moment that I would live in darkness forever. I felt absolute terror in my soul. [xi]

Sittser was later reminded that "the quickest way for anyone to reach the sun and the light of day is not to run west, chasing after the setting sun, but to head east, plunging into the darkness until one comes to the sunrise."[xii] He continues:

I discovered in that moment that I had the power to choose the direction my life would head, even if the only choice open to me, at least initially, was either to run from the loss or to face it as best I could. Since I knew that darkness was inevitable and unavoidable, I decided from that point on to walk into the darkness rather than try to outrun it, to let my experience of loss take me on a journey wherever it would lead, and to allow myself to be transformed by my suffering rather than to think I could somehow avoid it. I chose to run toward the pain, however falteringly, and to yield to the loss, though I had no idea at the time what that would mean. [xiii]

Sittser's words challenged us to take our grief and problems head-on—to proactively work through them, trying to make good and purpose come from our loss. Not that doing this mitigates the tragedy, but it often does make the emotional load easier to bear. If we can strive to face the darkness of loss on one hand, and learn to live with renewed vitality and gratitude on the other hand, then loss can function as a catalyst to transform and expand us. "It can lead us to God, the only One who has the desire and power to give us life." [xiv] With that being said, one of the most practical things we did to find comfort was to proactively lean into our grief, working through it, striving to make as much good as possible come from bad. In the first months after the accident, we produced the "Trust"

CD project, spent countless hours sharing our faith with others and embarked on the Lindsay-Grace Community Playground construction project. Seeing positive ripples of influence and encouragement as a result of our daughter's legacy lifted our spirits.

I don't want to give the impression that all the pain will go away indefinitely if one pours his heart out to God, gets good counsel and support, reads inspiring books and works proactively into grief. In fact, just last night at a worship concert at church, I saw a mother with her young blond head-banded daughter who reminded me of Lindsay-Grace. My tears started to flow, despite the joyful song that was being sung. I tried to pull myself together and will myself to stop. However, the tears kept coming, which surprised me, since I hadn't cried that hard about Lindsay-Grace in years. Nevertheless, overall, these aforementioned suggestions helped us a lot and, once again, we identified with Jerry Sittser:

> *Never have I felt so broken, yet never have I been so whole. Never have I been so aware of my weakness and vulnerability; yet never have I been so content and felt so strong. Never has my soul been more dead; yet never has my soul been more alive. What*

I once considered mutually exclusive—sorrow and joy, pain and pleasure, death and life—have become parts of a greater whole. My whole soul has been stretched. [xv]

Trusting God for Hope and Purpose

"God can do anything, you know, far more than you could ever imagine or guess or request in your wildest dreams! He does it not by pushing us around but by working within us, His Spirit deeply and gently within us" (Ephesians 3:20, MSG).

A year after Lindsay-Grace's death, Phil wrote a deeply heart-felt song called "Earthly Point of View." One particular line from the song reflects a lesson that we have learned:

> *Why did this happen to me? Was it me who sinned or someone else who caused this calamity? Then I heard you say, "No, my child, neither of these is true, but that the work of God be displayed in you."*

This expression of God is found in the Biblical story in John:

> As (Jesus) went along, He saw a man blind from birth. His disciples asked him, "Rabbi, who sinned, this man or his parents, that he was born blind?" [In other words, why did this terrible thing happen?] "Neither this man nor his parents sinned," said Jesus, "but this happened so that the works of God might be displayed in him" (John 9:1–3).

It's permissible to ask God "why"—in fact, Jesus asked, "why" as He was being crucified.[xvi] However, instead of dwelling on *why* bad things happen to us, we should ask, "For what purpose?" Nancy Guthrie writes, "The purpose in the blind man's suffering, your suffering, and my suffering is all the same: to display the glory of God. Every difficulty—from the minor irritation of a broken piece of crystal to the piercing pain of a broken relationship—God has allowed every one for the singular and supreme purpose of transforming your character into the likeness of His Son, thus glorifying Him."[xvii]

For one who doesn't have a relationship with God,

Idea of suffering so God may be glorified may id offensive or sadistic. For one who knows God, understanding the value in this purpose in the midst of a tragedy brings joy, peace and hope.

There has been a relevant story, by an unknown author, which has been circulating around the Internet for years.

Malachi 3:3 says: "He will sit as a Refiner and Purifier of silver." This verse puzzled some women in a Bible study and they wondered what this statement meant about the character and nature of God. One of the women offered to find out the process of refining silver and get back to the group at their next Bible study.

That week, the woman called a silversmith and made an appointment to watch him at work. She didn't mention anything about the reason for her interest beyond her curiosity about the process of refining silver.

As she watched the silversmith, he held a piece of silver over the fire and let it heat up. He explained that in refining silver, one needed to hold the silver in the middle of the fire where the flames were hottest as to burn away all the impurities.

The woman thought about God holding us in such a hot spot then she thought again about the verse that says: "He sits as a refiner and purifier of silver."

She asked the silversmith if it was true that he had to sit there in front of the fire the whole time the silver was being refined. The man answered that yes, he not only had to sit there holding the silver, but he had to keep his eyes on the silver the entire time it was in the fire. If the silver was left a moment too long in the flames, it would be destroyed. The woman was silent for a moment. Then she asked the silversmith, "How do you know when the silver is fully refined?" He smiled at her and answered, "Oh that's easy—when I see my image in it."

If today you are feeling the heat of the fire, remember that God has His eye on you and will keep watching you until He sees His image in you.[xviii]

Phil

Like in the story of the silver refiner, we wanted God's image in us. As followers of Jesus, we knew we wanted to follow His example. Just before He was arrested and crucified, Jesus prayed, "Father, if you are willing, take this cup from me; yet not my will, but yours be done" (Luke 22:42). This was the Son of God, and He knew His mission was to be sacrificed for the sins of the world. However, He asked for a way out, not wanting to endure the soon-coming horror. Jesus knew it would be agonizing. He knew He would be brutally murdered. He knew He would, for a period of time, be separated from His heavenly Father and so pleaded for another way, but ultimately, He knew His crucifixion would bring glory to God. That was more important than His own physical well-being. He willfully yielded His desires and entered into His suffering, opening the door for people to come to the Father. If Jesus was willing to enter suffering, trusting God for a higher purpose, then we, as His followers, must do the same.[xix]

It should be noted here that one might not always be able to make sense of heartaches and tragedies this side of heaven. The Lord promises to always be with us, but is not obligated to show us His purposes.

We made the conscious effort not to push too hard into the "why" of our loss. A truth that author John Eldredge has often articulated is "You can have understanding, or you can have God." This concept may be especially difficult for those who love God sincerely and enjoy serving in their churches but underneath it all, they expect God to improve their lives in return. In his book *Walking With God*, Eldredge calls this attitude A+B=C . . . "(A) believe in God, (B) be a good person, and (C) He will deliver the rest."[xx] Karen and I are living proof that this is *not* reality. We loved God before this—truly loved Him, served Him, did our best to walk with Him but then— January 18, 2003. However, the more we desired for God's image to be in us and to make His name great, the more opportunities He gave us to do just that. This brought us hope and satisfaction in the midst of our pain. Those followers of Jesus who are suffering must trust God to do what's right. *"For my thoughts are not your thoughts, neither are your ways my ways," declares the LORD. "As the heavens are higher than the earth, so are my ways higher than your ways and my thoughts than your thoughts" (Isaiah 55:8–9).*

Karen

God was trustworthy in preparing us for the biggest storm of our lives, and in comforting us in the midst of it. In addition, we noticed that the Lord could be trusted to give hope and a purpose through the storm. Even in the initial agonizing days after Lindsay-Grace's passing, we experienced a deep peace. We hurt a lot but, in a strange kind of way, my heart had a sense of hopeful anticipation. I sensed the power of the Holy Spirit preparing to explode from this situation like a racehorse getting ready to charge out of the starting gate. The Lord reiterated this impression the next morning after the accident when we went to church. There was a time in the service when individuals could write prayer requests, and in doing this, Phil and I beseeched the Lord to be glorified and to bring about good from the tragedy. Prayerfully we also lit a small candle and then snuffed the stick's feisty flame in the sand jar to extinguish the blaze. We later got this email from a friend of ours:

> After you and Phil lit a candle at church last Sunday, you both turned and walked away. (My husband) watched as the wick that you'd stuck in

*the sand leapt in the air about a foot and a half
high! Then the flame kept burning. The Lord was
there among us that day! His fire could not be put
out. And I'm convinced He will continue to fuel
your own flames as you continue your journey.*

Yes, the Spirit's flame from all this was not to be
quickly extinguished. There would be the joy and
privilege of seeing purpose revealed from Lindsay-
Grace's death. One example takes us back to the story
about the "Trust" CDs. We gave these away for free,
but accepted donations to build the Lindsay-Grace
Lazo Community Playground in the meadow behind
our church in Maryland. Ten and a half months after
the accident, amidst balloons and cakes and hundreds
of eager children and grown-ups, the purple ribbons
were cut to signify the official grand opening.

The journey to that day was an amazing one. Tens
of thousands of dollars had rolled in from "Trust"
CD donations, and construction and landscaping
businesses affiliated with the Association of Builders
and Contractors of Metro Washington donated
services, thus making the dream a reality. The
primary playground assembly day was scheduled to
take place on November 8, 2003. I was dismayed upon

learning this date because that was the weekend of our church's men's retreat, and all those strong guys wouldn't be around to lend a hand. If the construction timing had gone according to my plan, all the men from our church would have conveniently assembled this playground. However, I came to see that God's plan was much better. I was lamenting the problem to my friend Beth Friedman, who, in turn, offered help from her Oseh Shalom Synagogue congregation in Laurel, Maryland. We also ended up having a variety of "friends of friends" join us to lend a hand. The main construction day ended up being incredible. There were around sixty people from varied backgrounds and faiths (Christian, Jewish and Muslim) who labored together from sun-up to sundown, creating something that would bring joy to families all over the region. The Fox and CBS affiliate television stations covered the story of the playground on their evening news broadcasts. The heart-warming segments about a community coming together were inspirational and encouraged viewers with a sense of the good of humanity.

After countless hours of adjusting, bolt-tightening and riveting, the playground was ready to go on Sunday, November 30. Preceding the ribbon-cutting, at the conclusion of a worshipful church service, a musical video segment was included that showed slides of the construction efforts overlaid by video clips of my husband and me telling the playground story. During the part of the video segment that expressed the quote from author Nancy Guthrie that "it is no tragedy in being ushered quickly from this life to the next when that next life is spent in the presence of God,"[xxi] Phil's mother received a cell phone call. She learned that her husband, Phil's father, who had been very ill in the hospital, had just passed away. It was such a bittersweet morning. Even though we would miss Phil's beloved dad, we were relieved to know that he was released from his long-time suffering and we were encouraged by the thought that Lindsay-Grace and her dear, godly grandfather could smile together from heaven on such a momentous day.

Our daughter's passing has positively benefited not only local kids through the creation of a wonderful place to play, but also underprivileged children overseas who are being helped physically through gifts given in Lindsay-Grace's memory. After the playground had been paid for, additional donations totaled enough to start and maintain a relief program (in conjunction with World Relief) for poverty-

Lindsay-Grace Lazo Community Playground Dedication Day (2003)

stricken children in Sierra Leone, Africa.[xxii] This was desperately needed because following the end of that nation's violent ten-year civil war, half the country was traumatized with its tens of thousands of dead or wounded. After several years, World Relief's focus shifted to the problem of sex trafficking, and it handed over its child-development program to local volunteers. The model center that was started in part with the memorial gifts spawned similar programs in thirty-seven African villages!

Lives of children in other nations were also impacted in the aftermath of Lindsay-Grace's death. At her "Celebration of Life" service, we requested that, in lieu of buying memorial flowers, interested families go to the Compassion International[xxiii] website and choose a child to sponsor. Shortly thereafter, several impoverished children from around the world found hope through their new benefactors. In cooperation with local churches overseas, the sponsored young people were provided life-changing benefits such as nutritious snacks and meals, educational opportunities, health and hygiene training, medical check-ups, and the message of God's love. Some of our friends chose to be a blessing to a child in a different way: They donated a new red "Lindsay-Grace Lazo Wheelchair"[xxiv] to a disabled four-year-old child from Venezuela. For the first time in his life, this young boy was able to experience the freedom of mobility.

Over the years, we have received countless emails and notes from adults telling how their lives have been changed as a result of our daughter's passing. For example, in 2002, a friend had begun considering a relationship with the Lord and had started attending our church. However, having studied the book of Genesis in a Bible study, a major stumbling block for her was the question about why God would have tested Abraham, asking him to sacrifice his only son, Isaac. She was appalled to consider how a loving God could do such a thing.

Even though we didn't know each other well, she felt compelled to come to Lindsay-Grace's service and wrote me a letter shortly thereafter (excerpts follow):

> *At the service when Phil spoke of the time he went into Lindsay-Grace's room and listened to the story of Abraham and Isaac, it spoke to me on many different levels. I was comforted to know that someone with such an obvious deep faith wondered what choice he would make. The words he put to music really spoke to me with one word being the key—trust. It dawned on me at that moment . . . I FELT it for the very first time . . . I don't understand it but I must TRUST HIM . . . It has really helped me to accept that I won't understand everything in my journey to know Him but I should trust in Him, and accept Him in my life.*

It was surprising that her one major spiritual conflict was addressed in the "Trust" song that Phil had been inspired to write two years earlier.

Another woman, the mother of one of our daughter's classmates, went to the "Celebration of

Life" service and attended church for the first time the following Sunday. She signed up for the annual women's retreat on that first day, attended the retreat, received Christ into her heart and then eventually went to school to become an evangelist.

We were amazed to receive several typed, single-spaced, multi-paged letters and countless emails explaining how our girl's passing influenced people to examine their lives and prioritize what was truly important. The following are some excerpts that meant so much to us:

> *Lindsay-Grace is my hero today and always because she has saved my life. —MF*

> *I want you to know that your reaction to Lindsay-Grace's passing has had an overpowering and profound effect on me. I want so much to know Jesus in a way that would empower me to trust in Him so much that I could feel the assurance that you are feeling. I'm sure most of us are reconsidering our relationship with God as a result of your testimony. God is surely glorified and honored by the two of you.—SC*

It isn't often that the miracle of faith is put before our eyes to witness. Today was one such time. The courage, peace and unending faith shown by you and Phil was a true testament to what God has meant us to be. We thank you for inspiring all of us to be better people, to try harder to reach out to others and to fully treasure each moment given as a gift to us with our beloved family and friends. —CF

I have three children of my own (ages 6, 9 and 11) and your celebration today had a profound impact on me. I will be a better father, better husband and I will strengthen my family's relationship with God as a result. —JK

From time to time, fear and doubt can creep into my life and stop me from doing what God would want me to do. Since Lindsay-Grace's funeral, the story of Jairus' daughter and Jesus' words, "Don't be afraid, just believe" go through my mind frequently. They offer hope and strength in every aspect of my life and remind me that Jesus is there to show me the way.—LM

In addition to God bringing hope and purpose to many people at the memorial service, He has brought hope and purpose to Phil and me as well. We have had precious opportunities to spend hours with people who have encountered horrific life-altering circumstances. It has been an unexpected joy and privilege to be on the front lines with people battling grief, encouraging them in their darkest hours.

With the African endeavors, Compassion International sponsorships and "Trust" CDs (with our daughter's story) going out to five continents, it is exciting to ponder how God truly did have a wonderful plan for Lindsay-Grace. He used this young girl to bring change around the world.

Trusting God for the Future

"For I know the plans I have for you," declares the LORD,
"plans to prosper you and not to harm you,
plans to give you hope and a future" (Jeremiah 29:11).

Many people ask us about Doug and Bethany Smith, the parents of Mandy who was also killed in the accident. Doug, who was driving that green Jeep Cherokee, did mostly recover, despite being given a less than one-percent chance of survival. On that cold January day, after his crash into the trees, he was medivacked in critical condition to the University of Maryland Shock Trauma Center where he underwent many surgeries.

After about seven weeks, when Doug regained

consciousness, Phil and I were among his first visitors. We didn't stay long, but we wept together, reflecting on what had happened and realizing that our lives had been forever changed. The Lord gave us peace in assuring Doug that we knew it was an accident and telling him we forgave him. Despite counsel to sue from well-intentioned colleagues, we found much more satisfaction in going to court to release him from legal responsibility. Even though our income is modest and could have benefited from a financial payout in a court settlement, we sensed that suing would not be the means by which God would provide for us financially in the future. We trusted Him to take care of us in other ways.

Between the Shock Trauma Center and the Kernan Rehabilitation Hospital, Doug was hospitalized for around eleven weeks. He has no recollection of the crash or even the days preceding it, so the cause of the accident remains a mystery despite an extensive investigation. After nearly three years of surgeries, Doug's main long-term medical issues were the loss of sight in one eye and persistent MRSA infections.

Recently, Doug answered several questions for me:

Overall, how are you doing?

I am doing very well. Considering the extent of my initial injuries, I am doing miraculously.

How has God comforted you through all of this?

My faith in God and the knowledge of His love for me have been an elemental part of my recovery. The prayers that were said, the blessings I received and, most importantly, His clear intention that I had work yet to do here are, in my opinion, the reasons I am here.

Any other stories you can share with us?

There are many stories, but I think the one that strikes closest to home for us is the love and grace that you and Phil have shown me. It is something that surprises most people who hear my story. In your place, they do not know what they would have done, but they are always amazed at your ability to forgive.

Bethany, Mandy's mother, also relied on faith in God and support of family and friends to get her through the dark months of grieving her precious daughter's death and being a support to her hospitalized husband, all while mothering her five other young children. Because her life is so busy and she lives far from us, we don't keep in close contact. I do, however, see her many winters when I host the annual "Lindsay-Grace Day Reunion of Friends" that brings together the families of our daughter's closest classmates. Although it is always a bittersweet event for me, I love being with these growing young people and having a chance to reconnect with their parents.

God has had His hand not only on the Smiths but upon our family as well, continuing to give us peace and direction. The pendulum of our early emotions—sometimes feeling okay, then being blind-sided with pangs of grief—gradually lessened in extremes over time. Our sons, Zack and Brett, have, by God's grace, handled it well. Both have memories of their sister but have not suffered long-term ill effects The tragedy has not prevented them from living happy, productive lives, and through this they have continued to learn how God can bring good from bad. Their trust is in Christ, and their sister's passing has helped them build their faith on a solid foundation.

For many years after Lindsay-Grace's death, countless people encouraged us to write a book about our story. Deep in our hearts, Phil and I sensed that God wanted us to do that too. However, I pushed that idea to the back burner for many years as I struggled with how to end this memoir. I imagined the whole story being neatly tied up in a package that would bring the loss of our daughter "full circle"— like restoring a young female presence in our home by adopting a girl in need, developing a non-profit organization to help other parents who have lost children or perhaps becoming more fully available to speak to church or community groups. Recently, Phil and I were getting ready to give our presentation at a local church. During the last worship song before we went up on the platform, the insight struck me, "Our lives are not solely defined by what has happened to us with the accident and our whole story doesn't have to be wrapped up in the theme of our daughter's passing." I felt relieved, as a weight had been lifted from my heart. I always strove to have everything in our presentation relate directly to Lindsay-Grace's death before this realization came to me that life is about more than the death of our daughter. As that worship song continued, Phil and I expeditiously whispered back and forth, changing the direction of the end of our talk. Instead of just explaining how people's lives have been influenced in the years following the accident, we decided to talk about what the Lord taught us in those dark days and how that changed the direction of our own lives, taking us on unrelated adventures that we could never have imagined.

Lindsay-Grace's passing has set us on a deeper journey of trust than we had ever experienced before. Because we experienced God's faithfulness in His preparing us for her death and comforting us in those hard times, and His trustworthiness in giving us hope and purpose, we have been emboldened to just calmly "go with it" when our lives take different turns than we expect.

There are many stories to tell, but I will just share some of our favorite ones that show how God provided for us and blessed us in joyous, totally unexpected ways.

Two years after saying good-bye to Lindsay-Grace, Phil and I were at church when a staff member told us that a visiting couple wanted to talk with us. We were directed toward the front of the auditorium where we met Mr. and Mrs. C., who were the brother and sister-in-law of friends of ours. They were visiting from North Carolina and had visited our church one time before, on the day after Lindsay-Grace's accident. They had heard about us that Sunday and, when they arrived home, felt led by God to give us a financial gift. Separately, they prayed about this, and the Lord put the same amount on both their hearts: $10,000. So that morning they presented us a check with the wish for us to spend it on something for ourselves and not give it away. So we did. After paying some outstanding medical bills, we bought ourselves some much-needed furniture that we treasure to this day.

Another way that God proved Himself trustworthy was in a medical capacity. I'd known my friend Kristen Ruiz for eight years. In 2008, I learned that she was having some medical issues and needed a new kidney. This concerned me because I didn't want to see Kristen's kids lose her at such a young age. Even if they wouldn't lose her to death, they'd lose her to dialysis that would keep her alive but wouldn't allow her to live a normal life. So being fairly connected in our community, I sent out many emails to encourage individuals to step up and get tested for becoming living kidney donors. Of course, needing to set a good example, I was also tested. I was convinced I wouldn't be a match. Kristen, with her Italian roots, was medium-complexioned; I was blond and very fair. I assumed people have to be of the same ethnic background to be a match. Also, Kristen and I had different blood types. So, it seemed that I had nothing to worry about.

My original agenda worked. Several people were tested. However, there was one element that did not go according to my plan: I was the only one who ended up being a match!

I was out grocery shopping when the transplant coordinator called me on my cell phone. Needless to say, upon hearing that I was a compatible donor for Kristen, I was taken aback. She told me that Kristen had not yet been informed, so if I wanted to decline I could, and no one would ever know. After hastily saying, "I'll get back to you," I disconnected from the transplant coordinator's call, instantly called Phil with the news, checked out with my purchases and went home to think.

Back in the quiet sanctity of our family room, I plopped down into our recliner with my Bible on my lap. The verse that had been rattling around in my head since getting the call was John 15:13, "Greater love has no one than this: to lay down one's life for one's friends." I went to the Scriptures, and reread the preceding verse with Jesus' words, "My command is this: Love each other as I have loved you." Even though I'd read this passage countless times, it hit me like a ton of bricks: Jesus is not just saying, "It would be really nice if you gave your all for your friend." He was commanding it. This sealed the deal. Within moments of getting home, the decision was made. If I call Jesus my Lord, I must be willing to do anything He wants me to do. I need to trust God with all of this. Phil and I prayed about it then contacted the transplant coordinator to tell her I would participate in the transplant. Next, I made the call to Kristen. She was having a rough day, and we engaged in small talk for the first few minutes. When I got around to telling her the news, she just wept.

The next two months were filled with all the necessary testing to secure my clearance for the surgery. It was actually a blessing to get this extremely thorough check-up. I had lots of blood analyses, urine tests, X-rays, an electrocardiogram, CT scan, psychological exams and other tests. Our family didn't have very comprehensive medical insurance, so this was a fantastic way to get every part of my body thoroughly examined for free.

I considered kidney donation as an adventure and didn't have second thoughts until a couple of months later when I was wheeled into the operating room and had one of those *"What in the world am I doing?"* moments. My heart sank as I saw the bright white sterile room with the lights, surgical equipment, masked and scrubbed physicians and nurses all gathered around a narrow, slightly-padded silver gurney on which I would soon be lying. This scenario had seemed so far off for so long, but now it was actually here. The next few hours in that cool, sterile room would be all about me. No turning back now. The friendly anesthesiologist came to my side and performed his duties.

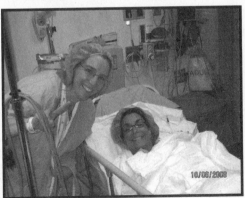

Karen and Kristen before the Transplant Surgery (2008)

Seemingly, a moment later, I awoke in a curtained-off section of a large recovery room with a huge bandage patch on my left side. It was surreal to think that my body had been invaded for several hours, but I hadn't even been aware of it. I felt gassy and tired, but other than that, pretty normal. After my family members and dear friend Debbie Hoover checked in on me, an orderly eventually wheeled me upstairs to my room where I could sleep off the rest of the anesthesia.

In the morning, I wasn't in pain and felt fine. I walked next door to see my friend Kristen, who had come through her surgery with flying colors. Her face looked different than it had the previous day. Yesterday, her complexion was pale with a yellowish hue; today it looked as if she had been out in the sun. The transplant was a big deal for Kristen, but it wasn't as much a big deal for me. Her road to full recovery was longer than mine, but I'm happy to report that, at this writing, she is doing very well. Today I have a few hardly-noticeable scars, but also the inexpressible joy and deep satisfaction in being chosen to give this priceless gift. God was trustworthy in providing me with valuable, thorough medical exams and blessing me with one of the most amazing experiences of my life.

Phil

Another surprising adventure that God took us on involved my job search and our family's finding a new home. I had enjoyed working in the sports broadcasting field since the early 1990s. However, for a season in 2008 there was not much media production work available for me, so it seemed obvious to pursue a new line of employment. A few months later I accepted a regular job as a producer/engineer for a Redskins football television show, but decided to still investigate a career change.

For the previous ten years, I had served as a volunteer worship leader at our church. More recently I had also been working as the part-time worship leader with a newly founded local congregation. Since many people have told me that I have a pastoral heart and am gifted at music ministry, I thought becoming a worship pastor would give me a meaningful career change. Having never been a paid full-time worship leader before, I wouldn't be an extremely strong candidate "on paper." So we knew God would have to open the doors with connections to make this happen.

Phil and his Guitar (2009)

Sure enough, the opportunities came. Through mutual friends and online church job postings, I had several meaningful and very promising conversations with senior pastors and search committees. However, no job offers materialized.

I was discouraged, yet confident that the Lord was working with my best interests at heart. We continued to trust God for our future. However, after over a year of close calls, our family decided to move from Maryland to Northern Virginia because the commute to my regular job was so long and expensive (with gas and tolls). A community church that we liked a lot was near my place of employment. So we thought we could move close-by so I could keep my job with the Redskins while building into the church as a volunteer musician.

Not long after we put our house on the market and started our search for a Northern Virginia home, I answered a phone call that set off an unexpected sequence of events. The call was from the senior pastor of a church where I had been a finalist for a worship leader position a year earlier. Apparently, the man they hired had not worked out. The church staff was seeking an interim worship pastor for six months while the search team could perform a more extensive search. After much conversation and prayer, I accepted this position. Getting the experience and the extra paycheck would be a big help. One exciting prospect was that after the church got to know me, they might offer me the full-time position later in the fall. So a few weeks later, I started this job. Because this church was in Maryland, it wouldn't make sense to move to Virginia right away. It seemed wiser to wait to see if I was offered the full-time worship pastor position. If I did, we would move closer to the church. If I didn't, we would stick to the original plan, move to Northern Virginia and, hopefully, plug into the other church there. We were just about to take our house off the market when we got a fantastic offer we just couldn't refuse. However, we had to be out of our home in a month.

Karen found an attractive and reasonably priced little dollhouse-looking rental home on a wooded half-acre that had just become available in Point of Rocks, Maryland, halfway between my two jobs. Within weeks, we put many of our belongings in storage and moved with mostly just the essentials. After all, we thought we would be in the rental home for only a few months.

My time as the interim worship pastor went well and the feedback was very positive. I did my best to make the music presentation excellent each Sunday and added creative elements to the service such as a variety of multimedia clips and hued lighting. I went through the application process for the full-time position just as the other applicants did. The day came for me to meet with the staff for my final interview. "Are you nervous?" Karen asked. She thought it was surprising that my response was, "The thing I'm most nervous about is if they offer me the job." Although working at the church was a joyous, valuable experience, I was second-guessing if leading worship every Sunday in a paid position was what I was being called to do. In addition, we were not totally convinced that this church was the right fit for our family. I prayed for clarity for my future, and God answered my prayer. The final interview was short and sweet, basically, "We have narrowed our search to two final candidates, and you are not one of them." So once again a job offer did not materialize.

We were surprised but we were okay with the outcome. I decided not to pursue any more full-time worship-leader jobs. I sensed I have this gifting and I enjoy leading worship, but preferred doing it only on a part-time basis. In addition, we sensed that our family needed to settle somewhere. Our son Zack had started high school and we wanted to give him some stability. Having been in our rental home four months, we needed to figure out where we should finally put down our roots. By this time, we had fallen in love with the bedroom community that had become like home to us. The kids really liked their schools, the home prices were reasonable, my commute to my regular job was cut in half, and the small-town atmosphere didn't have the hectic pace of life that we had experienced for so long. We felt like we were on vacation living in Point of Rocks. The community is situated on the Potomac River with its historic C&O Canal towpath. There are lots of places to take in breath-taking scenery on bike rides and hikes. We could admire sunrise over the mountains each morning, hear the trains in the distance, delight in seeing horses and cows grazing in nearby pastures and gaze at the stars at night. It was a breath of fresh air living here, literally and figuratively.

So, after weeks of negotiations, we signed a contract to build a house there in the community that we had once thought would be temporary. This was a dream come true. We didn't think we'd have an opportunity any time soon to do this. However, this brand new house cost less than the price for which we had sold our previous house, so it just made sense. If it hadn't been for my worship pastor job search and the lack of job offers, we would never have thought to settle there. We absolutely love it now and are thankful for the friendships and opportunities that have come our way.

We found an outreach-oriented, friendly, solid Bible-teaching church where I have happily plugged into the worship team as a volunteer. It was interesting that about two-and-a-half years after we started attending this church, a full-time worship director job became available there. It gave me an opportunity for a gut-check: Had I just "settled in defeat" by discontinuing my worship director position search? Since our family is already part of this church community, would I want to pursue this full-time position since we wouldn't have to move anywhere? After much soul-searching, I decided I was at peace about keeping my current job and continuing to serve on the worship team as a volunteer, not as a full-time employee. This felt right for us, and although my employment search didn't conclude as we had initially thought it would, it took all of those steps and roadblocks and opportunities to get us to where we are today. We are so happy and at peace.

Karen

Coming full-circle back to this book's original theme of stories about Lindsay-Grace, we had two more incredible experiences that encouraged us eleven years after her passing. The first was an experience shared with us by one of Lindsay-Grace's friends, Val. During her middle and high school years, Val went to a lot of funerals, including the services of Lindsay-Grace and another fourteen-year-old family friend. These deaths had a negative impact on her life, and her social relationships suffered. When Val graduated from high school, she decided she was not ready to leave home; instead, she opted for community college. She also participated in therapy to help her talk out her worries. After two years, Val decided she was ready to move to a residential university. The first days were so much harder than she had anticipated, and being away from her parents and living with strangers was difficult.

Here is the rest of the story in Val's words:

> *Every night since January 18, 2003, I prayed that Lindsay-Grace was safe and that I would see her just one more time to say good-bye. Even though it had been eleven years, I never gave up asking to see her. The night before my first day of classes, I was so nervous. I said my usual prayers and went to bed, but this was no normal night. In a vivid dream, I saw Lindsay-Grace. We were both kids again and we were sitting on her bed in her room. She was in some type of sports uniform. She told me to come play with her for a little bit. We played and then she took me to her bedroom window and*

told me to look outside. There, sitting in a field, were Karen, Phil, Zack and Brett and a crowd of familiar and unfamiliar faces. Lindsay-Grace told me that they are all the people she is watching over. She took me back to her bed to sit down and she told me that it was time to be strong and that it was time to move on. She handed me a friendship bracelet she had made and said, "Keep me with you." It was then time to say goodbye. She shook my hand and hugged me and said, "We will meet again. Tell my parents this story and that I love them and that I am safe and having fun." I said goodbye and then woke up with tears rolling down my face and with the calmest and most relaxed feeling. I can't even describe it. God sent Lindsay-Grace at the time I needed her the most. I will never forget that moment. It truly was precious. I hope this story brings a smile because it gives me a smile every time I think about it.

Val's story meant so much to us. We felt as though Lindsay-Grace had communicated with us and confirmed that she is alive and well and happy. There were two details about her account that got our attention. First, it was interesting that Lindsay-Grace initially shook hands with her friend in the dream. We always encouraged our kids to be confident enough to shake people's hands. Second, I asked Val what color uniform Lindsay-Grace was wearing in the dream, and she said green. Lindsay-Grace passed away in her green basketball uniform. Val had no way of knowing that.

Another "God-thing" we experienced occurred on the weekend that I was researching our options to get this book published. Driving to church, we first saw a bouquet of a dozen purple and white balloons in the weeds on the side of the road, and then five miles farther we saw a girl's pink birthday Mylar balloon stuck on the guardrail. There were no homes anywhere near these sites. We had never before seen balloons on this familiar drive, but their presence on that day was significant because it was what would have been our daughter's twentieth birthday. It was amazing that Lindsay-Grace loved balloons, and purple was her favorite color! Also, she loved the style of flowers on the Mylar one. (In fact, these cartoon-like blooms are engraved on her headstone.) We picked up the stray balloons on the way home so we could continue to marvel at their appearance. Even though the big bunch had partially popped and deflated by that time, seeing them was such a joy to us, and we thank God for this birthday surprise.

The Miraculous Birthday Balloons (2014)

These are just a few of the many recent stories of how the Lord has shown Himself trustworthy in encouraging us and putting us in positive circumstances that we could never have imagined. We trusted God for our future even though we didn't know what His next move would be. There have been so many times along the way that we thought we knew what God was going to do, but then He showed us He had something different and better in mind. The Lord can do the same for each of us.

With all this being said, it begs one final question: how exactly does one trust God for preparation, comfort, hope, purpose and the future? I am not a theologian and will not attempt to embark on a scholarly discourse about how to do this. However, I'd be remiss in not briefly coming back around to our friend Abraham (formerly called Abram) whose story started this whole tale of trust for us. In the book of Genesis, God invited Abram on a journey and promised His blessings:

> *The LORD had said to Abram, "Go from your country, your people and your father's household to the land I will show you. I will make you into a great nation, and I will bless you; I will make your name great, and you will be a blessing. I will bless those who bless you, and whoever curses you I will curse; and all peoples on earth will be blessed through you." So Abram went, as the LORD had told him (Genesis 12: 1–4a).*

This patriarch believed God, took Him at His word and acted on it, putting "feet on his faith" (even though Abram could not fully understand). In the same way, we must believe that our God is a loving God who has a plan for us. (See a few proof verses near the end of this chapter.) Then, in considering Abram's example, we should live our lives in such a way that shows we're obviously "stepping out" and following a higher authority for our lives. In other words, if we have true faith and trust, we, like Abram, should have our lives reflect that. May each of us be challenged by this query that has been given down through the years: "If following God were a crime, would there be enough evidence to convict you?"

Phil

As Karen and I struggled to discern God's plan for our lives after Lindsay-Grace's passing, we "stepped out" to try different paths. We started a non-profit organization to raise funds for memorial projects for lost loved ones. As much as we loved being a part of making good come from bad, we eventually realized we did not enjoy continually soliciting for donations. So we discontinued this organization after a few years. Another path we considered was adoption. Our hearts were not leaping at this possibility but, nevertheless, we participated in orphan hosting while telling God to stir our hearts if this is what we were supposed to be doing long-term. Our hosted student was not available for adoption at that time, so we had a non-pressured and worthwhile experience. It was a joy to see him grow in faith, confidence and life skills. However, we sensed adoption was not what God wanted our family to pursue at that time. Instead, we would continue to care for orphans through overseas sponsorships. Even though we tried some experiences that ultimately didn't become long-term aspects of our lives, it was beneficial to experience these things. They helped clarify our desire to be a blessing by sharing our story and encouraging others to trust God, especially when life is not going as planned.

In "stepping out," it is important to go forth expectantly, open to what God will do. Recently, on a ministry dialog website, a participant, Fletch, articulated this well:

> *Now I'm trying to just "show up" and see what God is up to rather than doing or not doing based on what I expect will or will not happen. Perhaps if I give God the option to determine things, rather than trying to predict the results of my actions, I may be in a very different relationship with God. This could have a big effect on my life.*

I like to look at this as an attempt at control. The more I try to control the outcome of things, the less these things may actually turn out the way I want. I need to cede control and my expectations to God. He will often work things out favorably for me but not always the way I expected them to be worked out. When the Lord told Abram to leave his country, his people and his father's household and to go to a land He would show him, God didn't tell Abram where he was going, how he would get there or what he would do to make a living. God did tell Abram that He would bless him, make him a great nation, and that all the nations of the world would be blessed because of him. Basically, the Lord was telling Abram, "Trust Me." God didn't tell him how, but He came through with all that He promised. The Bible says, "So Abram went, as the LORD had told him," and God took care of the rest on His timetable and in His way. Abram just had to "show up."

Karen

We do not want to imply that there are always easy answers to heartbreak. Life can still be difficult even as we trust God to work out all things for our ultimate good. With that said, here are some tips to remember when we are trusting God.

- How does one start to trust? Praise God and find something for which to give Him thanks. This will get your heart in the right place to start trusting Him.

"Enter his gates with thanksgiving
and his courts with praise;
give thanks to him and praise his name" (Psalm 100:4).

"Give thanks in all circumstances; for this is God's will for
you in Christ Jesus" (1 Thessalonians 5:18).

- Make your relationship with the Lord your top priority. The closer your relationship is with Him, the easier it is to find and follow His path for you.

"Your word is a lamp for my feet, a light on my path"
(Psalm 119:105).

(Jesus said) "I am the vine; you are the branches. If you remain
in me and I in you, you will bear much fruit; apart from me
you can do nothing. If you do not remain in me, you are like
a branch that is thrown away and withers; such branches are

picked up, thrown into the fire and burned" (John 15:5–6).

- While believing, continually look to God and remember to ask Him to work things out for you. Don't just *think* about wanting God to work things out for you.

"If any of you lacks wisdom, you should ask God, who gives generously to all without finding fault, and it will be given to you. But when you ask, you must believe and not doubt, because the one who doubts is like a wave of the sea, blown and tossed by the wind. That person should not expect to receive anything from the Lord" (James 1:5–7).

"Trust in the LORD with all your heart and lean not on your own understanding; in all your ways submit to him, and he will make your paths straight" (Proverbs 3:5–6).

- What if you don't *feel* like God is going to help you? Sometimes there is a disconnect between our minds knowing that God can help us, and our hearts believing that He will help us. If the Lord shows you a promise from the Scriptures, tell God that your head knows He can fulfill this promise. If your heart is unconvinced, ask Him to help your heart to believe it as well. Keep practicing this exercise; in time your heart will catch up with your head.

"I do believe; help me overcome my unbelief" (Mark 9:24).

"And we know that in all things God works for the good of those who love him, who have been called according to his purpose" (Romans 8:28).

- It is a good idea to have a list of "go-to" Bible verses to encourage you in times of need. There are many book and Internet resources that list selections of Scripture that relate to various types of struggles. These are two promises that have meant the most to Phil and me:

"The God of all grace, who called you to his eternal glory in Christ, after you have suffered a little while, will himself restore you and make you strong, firm and steadfast" (1 Peter 5:10).

However, as it is written: "What no eye has seen, what no ear has heard, and what no human mind has conceived"— the things God has prepared for those who love him—

these are the things God has revealed to us by his Spirit"
(1 Corinthians 2:9 – 10a).

- Remember: you won't always sense God's presence, but that doesn't mean He isn't there. He loves you!

"Be strong and courageous. Do not be afraid or terrified because of them, for the LORD your God goes with you; he will never leave you nor forsake you" (Deuteronomy 31:6).

"For I am convinced that neither death nor life, neither angels nor demons, neither the present nor the future, nor any powers, neither height nor depth, nor anything else in all creation, will be able to separate us from the love of God that is in Christ Jesus our Lord" (Romans 8:38–39).

- Sometimes you may find yourself at a fork in the road and may not know which path to take. I believe that sometimes God gives us more than one good option. Check your motives; if they are God-honoring, you can most likely have the freedom to choose either way. However, be sure to check in with God as you go along, asking Him to get you back on the best path if you go astray.

"When you ask, you do not receive, because you ask with wrong motives, that you may spend what you get on your pleasures" (James 4:3).

"To humans belong the plans of the heart, but from the LORD comes the proper answer of the tongue. All a person's ways seem pure to them, but motives are weighed by the LORD. Commit to the Lord whatever you do, and He will establish your plans. . . . In their hearts humans plan their course, but the Lord establishes their steps" (Proverbs 16:1–3, 9).

- Be patient and open-minded when surprises and storms come your way. Nothing can happen to you that is not filtered through God's love for you. Your Lord knows what He's doing and He can redeem every heartache that you ever experience.

(The LORD says) "As the heavens are higher than the earth, so are my ways higher than your ways and my thoughts than your thoughts" (Isaiah 55:9).

"'For I know the plans I have for you,' declares the LORD, 'plans to prosper you and not to harm you, plans to give you hope and a future'" (Jeremiah 29:11).

Phil

At this writing, Lindsay-Grace has been gone for twelve years. Life marches on. Her portraits hang throughout our house and not a day goes by that we don't think of her. Tears occasionally come, but not as often as they did when our loss was so raw. We thank God for how He has provided preparation, comfort, hope and purpose in our lives. Our days are marked with deep peace and excitement about trusting the Lord for our unseen future. We love God even more than we did before our loss. By His grace, we are well and we are happy.

If we let Him, the Lord will take us places here on earth we never imagined, use us in ways we never dreamed, through circumstances we would have never asked for. In trusting God with all your heart, we pray you will experience life to the full, as can only come from Him.

Epilogue

(Jesus says) "Therefore, everyone who hears these words of mine and puts them into practice is like a wise man who built his house on the rock. The rain came down, the streams rose, and the winds blew and beat against that house; yet it did not fall, because it had its foundation on the rock" (Matthew 7:24–25).

It is not ideal to start building a house on solid ground when the storm is already on the horizon. The house, or your life, is stronger when it has already been established prior to the storm. A life built on Christ's solid foundation will weather and withstand life's heartaches and tragedies. Even in the midst of our deepest sorrows, our heavenly Father will stay with us and shine through us if we let Him. We will not be destroyed and can become better for our difficulties instead of bitter.

The storms of life will come. You will face loss. Everyone faces loss. Maybe you will have to deal with the death of someone close. Or perhaps someday you will experience the death of a dream—of lifelong love, financial security, successful children, health and safety. We would strongly encourage you to build your life on a solid foundation—a vital relationship with Jesus Christ—before the inevitable storms of life come your way. How do you do this? Here's the way *The Message* version of the Bible explains it:

> *It's the word of faith that welcomes God to go to work and set things right for us. This is the core of our preaching. Say the welcoming word to God—"Jesus is my Master"—embracing, body and soul, God's work of doing in us what He did in raising Jesus from the dead. That's it. You're not "doing" anything; you're simply calling out to God, trusting him to do it for you. That's salvation. With your whole being, you embrace God setting things right, and then you say it, right out loud: "God has set everything right between him and me" (Romans 10:9–10).*

If you invite Jesus into your life and want to grow stronger in your relationship with Him, do as you would when you want to get to know a new friend: make it a priority to spend time with Him. Talk with Him (pray). Hear from Him (read and study the Bible). Hang out with His friends (get involved with a community of believers). The Scriptures tell us, "He who believes in Him [Jesus] shall not be disappointed" (1 Peter 2: 6, NASB). That is God's promise.

If you are already walking with God, we encourage you to practice trusting Him more and more. Trusting God is like exercising a muscle: to become strong, you must work through increased degrees of strain and stress. Putting the tips into practice from the previous chapter, start trusting the Lord in simple circumstances. When you are running late and get stuck at a red light; when your significant other is not returning your phone call; when your child is not invited to a neighbor's birthday party; when the boss needs to have a word with you; when any inconvenience comes your way, tell God that you believe He can work everything together for good (see Romans 8:28) and that you trust Him. Even if your heart does not believe it right away, make a practice of articulating that truth out loud and watch what the Lord will do.

How can you know how you are doing? I

encourage you to do an honest reality check every once in a while: Can you trust God if you do not sense His presence? Can you trust Him when there seems to be no reason for your heartaches? How would you respond if your most precious possession were taken away?

Another excellent practice is to examine yourself when problems come. In the words of Nancy Guthrie in her book *Holding on to Hope:*[XXV]

> *When our skin is pricked by a thorn, what comes out is what is inside: blood. When our lives are pricked by difficulty, what comes out is what's inside. For some of us, it is selfishness, pride, bitterness, and anger that come seeping out. For others, it is the fruit of the Spirit—love, joy, peace, patience, kindness, goodness, faithfulness, gentleness, and self-control (Galatians 5:22–23).*

What is inside of you?

The story is told of an art center contest that offered a major cash prize for the best painting depicting the "Essence of Peace." Entries submitted included the traditional millennial kingdom depiction of the slumbering "Lion and the Lamb" and the tranquil portrayal of a "Morning Meadow." However, the painting that won was a real surprise. Titled "In the Midst of the Storm," it depicted an eagle's nest perched on the edge of a 10,000-foot cliff. "A storm raged, threatening to destroy everything in its path, with lightning, thunder, and treacherous winds. Two tiny eaglets slept soundly, snuggled in the soft down taken from their mother's breast. Their parents sat close by watching over them. Oblivious to the danger around them, these eagle fledglings knew only contentment and trust."[xxvi]

Peace is not just the absence of a storm but rest in the middle of the storm. Our prayer for you, our reader, is to experience the peace that God promises if you are resting where you ought to be. If you would like to share your stories with us or if we can be of assistance to you, please contact us via our website WWW.TRUSTSTORY.ORG.

In His grip,
Phil and Karen Lazo

Acknowledgments

Thank you

To our family—the Lazos, Jessens, Vislays, Corkrans, and Joneses—who have supported us every step of the way.

To our dear friends and church family—especially Debbie Hoover, Chris and Elaine Hill, Patti Tuttle, Bev Zalewski, Jeff Miller, Mike Baumgardner, Andrew Bieber and Jennifer Moore—who have walked this journey with us and faithfully loved us in such practical ways.

To Brian McLaren, who went above and beyond the call of duty as a pastor and a friend, and who gave us a lot of insights included in this book. His encouragement has meant the world to us.

To Bryan Anderson (Exnihilo Music) for doing a fantastic job producing and engineering our

songs "Trust," "Earthly Point of View" and "Hope."
EXNIHILO-MUSIC.COM

To Blair Anderson (A Visual Planet) who created our stunning "Trust" CD cover art. AVISUALPLANET.COM

To Zack, Brett, Rebecca, Kelsey, Anne, Bethany, Doug, Chris, Keith, Bryan, Tori, Pattie, Bonnie, Deana, Jana, Beth, Mr. and Mrs. C, Kristen, Val, Fletch and those unnamed for sharing their personal stories and insights. Their contributions to this book really make God look good!

To Lindsay-Grace's friends who have continued to share their lives with us over the years—Ashley, Carley, Daniel, Emily, Justin, Kelsey, Lee, Mariah, Matthew, Natalie, Rebecca, Sadie, Sarah, Tori and Will.

To the band Northbound for their dedication and skill in recording the trilogy of songs on our TRUSTSTORY. ORG website.

To the churches in the United States and abroad who have invited and encouraged us to share and develop our story.

Acknowledgments

To Chandler Birch, Madison Wasinger, Becca Mackay, Believers Press and Christian Writers Guild who helped us make this dream of publication a reality.

To the proofreaders who took the time to give us specific corrections, suggestions, and feedback. This book is better than what it would have otherwise been, thanks to them.

Caitlin Anselmo
Caroline Bair
Robin Bair (BUB!)
Mike Baumgardner
Dede Corkran
Bryan Doyle
Elaine Hill
Debbie Hoover
Marilyn Jessen
Jeffrey Jones
Daria Knupp
June Lazo
Katrina Long
Brian McLaren
Cheri Vislay
David O. Stewart and The Writer's Center's Fact-Based Narrative Workshop Participants (Bethesda, MD)

Most of all, we thank God for the privilege of participating in and telling this story. We give Him the glory for all He has done!

Endnotes

i Frank Peretti, "Trust." *Mr. Henry's Wild & Wacky Totally True Bible Stories*. (Nashville, TN: Thomas Nelson, 2000).

ii "For God so loved the world, that he gave his only Son, that whoever believes in him shall not perish, but have eternal life" (John 3:16, NIV).

iii Mark 5:21–43, Matthew 9:18–26, Luke 8:40–56

iv The poem "For a Little Time" by Edgar Guest was modified to reflect a daughter's passing (instead of the original son).

v Isaiah 55:8–9

vi Psalm 139:7–12

vii Matthew 5:14–16

viii Jesus, Inspirational Films, Inc., (San Clemente, CA, 1980).

ix Lon Solomon, *Brokenness: How God Redeems Pain and Suffering* (Potomac, MD: Red Door Press, 2005), 24.

x Ibid., 58.

xi Jerry Sittser, *A Grace Disguised: How the Soul Grows Through Loss, Expanded Edition* (Grand Rapids, MI: Zondervan, 2004), 41.

xii Ibid., 42.

xiii Ibid., 42.

xiv Ibid., 200.

xv Ibid., 199.

xvi Matthew 27:46, Mark 15:34

xvii Nancy Guthrie, *Holding on to Hope* (Wheaton, IL: Tyndale House, 2002), 43.

xviii Malachi 3:3 says: "He will sit as a Refiner and Purifier of ..," HTTP://WWW.SALTANDLIGHTGROUP.COM/PDFS/FREEDOM_SILVER_REFINED.PDF (accessed May 15, 2005).

xix "Then Jesus said to his disciples, 'Whoever wants to be my disciple must deny themselves and take up their cross and follow me. For whoever wants to save their life will lose it, but whoever loses their life for me will find it. What good will it be for someone to gain the whole world, yet forfeit their soul? Or what can anyone give in exchange for their soul?'"

(Matthew 16:24–26, NIV).

xx John Eldredge, *Walking with God: Talk to Him. Hear from Him. Really.* (Nashville, TN: Thomas Nelson, 2008), 8.

xxi Guthrie, 65.

xxii HTTP://WORLDRELIEF.ORG

xxiii HTTP://WWW.COMPASSION.COM

xxiv HTTP://WWW.WHEELCHAIRFOUNDATION.ORG, WHEELCHAIR #89133

xxv Guthrie, 17.

xxvi Essence of Peace—Dr. Sharon Schuetz, HTTP://DRSHARONSCHUETZ.COM/?P=364 (accessed November 2, 2012).